Born to Write

The Remarkable Lives of Six Famous Authors

CHARIS COTTER

 annick press
toronto + new york + vancouver

Image Credits

Contents

Acknowledgments

I began writing this book in Newfoundland in the summer of 2008, with the ongoing support of my many friends there. Thanks to Colleen and Zoe for cooking delicious suppers while I wrote, thanks to Tom and Rick for lending me their house to write in when the renovations got too noisy, and thanks to Sue and Wayne for their wood donations. Maureen Snow at the Carbonear Library helped me master the mysteries of the inter-library loan system so I could get the books I needed. Back on the mainland, I was indebted to Denise Anderson at Scholastic for helping me get in touch with Christopher Paul Curtis. I am very grateful for Christopher's generous contribution of his time, his stories, his photographs, and his mother's phone number! Leslie Curtis kept me laughing with her family stories and gave me her valuable mother's insight into the "king of mischief." Thanks to Evelyn Cotter for her early reading of the manuscript and her thoughtful contributions to the E.B. White chapter, and thanks to Graham Cotter for his insights into Madeleine L'Engle. Elizabeth MacLeod kindly helped me out with some questions I had about L. M. Montgomery. A heartfelt thank you to school librarian Teri Evangelista for her input and support, and another to my editor, John Sweet, for nursing both me and the manuscript along. Thanks to Karen Hunter for her patient and extensive picture research. And it's always a pleasure to work with Sheryl Shapiro, both for her inspired designs and her cheerful, flexible attitude, and thanks also to everyone at Annick for all their help at a very busy time. This book was written with support from the Ontario Arts Council.

For my mother, who taught me how to write, and my father, who read me the Narnia books, one chapter at a time.

—C.C.

Echoes of Childhood

If you love reading books, you know what it is like to lose yourself in a story. Your bedroom drops away and you're in the world of the book, side by side with the hero or heroine. Your ticket to those other worlds depends on the strength of your imagination and the power of the words you're reading. The best writers scoop you up and take you on a ride that ends only on the last page of the book.

To create this kind of magic, a writer needs a very special kind of imagination. Most children haven't yet learned to put limits on their daydreams; they can easily imagine flying, or skipping through time, or enjoying magical powers. Children who grow up to be writers have something extra. Along with a vivid imagination, they often have a driving need to create an imaginary world that's an improvement on the one they live in. Nearly all of the writers in this book had to endure hardships in their childhoods—parents who died or abandoned them, isolation and bullying at school, or simply a lack of friends or grown-ups who understood and loved them. But somehow these children found the time and space to create their own secret worlds, which were much more intense and satisfying than their everyday lives.

And when they grew up, instead of forgetting what it felt like to be a child, they remembered, and put it into their books. Fragments of their childhood selves echo through their writing: the intriguing attic tunnel in C. S. Lewis's *The Magician's Nephew*, Meg's itchy feeling of never fitting in at school in Madeleine L'Engle's *A Wrinkle in Time*, the ghostly clock in L. M. Montgomery's *The Story Girl*.

What happens to people makes them who they are. This book tells the stories of how six extraordinary children transformed their childhood struggles into spellbinding bedtime reading for kids everywhere.

Power of your imagination

Wri

If you love reading books, you know what it is like to lose yourself in a story. Your bedroom drops away and you're in the world of the book, side-by-side with the hero or heroine. Your ticket to those other worlds depends on the power of your imagination and the power of the words you're reading. The best writers scoop you up and take you on a ride that only ends on the last page of the book.

to create the kind of magic a writer needs a very special kind of imagination

Lucy Maud Montgomery
(1874–1942)

The Thin Veil

Maud sat at her little desk in her bedroom reading over the story she had completed the evening before. Outside her window the orchard was alight with apple blossoms dancing in the pale spring sunshine. But for once she was indifferent to the siren call of the outdoors. "The Graves" was her best story yet. It told the sad tale of a woman married to a traveling preacher who went from town to town across Canada. She had nine children and they all succumbed, one by one, to deadly illnesses. Maud had described each deathbed scene and each wretched funeral. After reading the final, heart-wrenching scene at the graveyard overlooking the Pacific Ocean, Maud raised her head and looked out the window through a mist of tears.

"It's good," she thought. "Just as good as a story in Godey's Lady's Book." Now she saw the apple trees and the hill field stretching up beyond them. A feeling of happiness rose up from her toes, as if she was a glass being filled with red raspberry cordial. She leapt to her feet. She had to get outside and run, down the field path to the shore, somewhere the sky would open up and hold this joy that was bursting through her skin.

"I'm going to be a writer," she repeated to herself as she clattered down the stairs, "I'm going to be a writer and be famous all over the world. I'm going to be a writer…"

"Maud, don't forget to feed those chickens before breakfast," called her grandmother from the kitchen. "It will be ready in five minutes."

Maud gave a cluck of impatience but obeyed, dashing through the kitchen and out into the yard. She hauled open the door to the granary.

"Catkin!" she called. "Pussy-willow!" She snatched the old basket from the shelf and began filling it with chicken feed. "Where are my pussycats this morning?"

A shadow darted past her out the door. Catkin, she decided. "Pussy-willow!" she called again. "Where are you Puss?"

She locked the kittens in the granary every night because Gyp, the dog, was forever worrying them, and Grandma wouldn't allow cats in the house.

A tiny miaow came from farther inside the granary. That didn't sound like Pussy-willow. He had a loud voice and not a shy bone in his body. Maud followed the cry.

The kitten lay on his side, a line of foam dribbling from his mouth. He tried to raise his head when he saw Maud, but he was too feeble. She dropped the basket of feed and fell to her knees, scooping him into her arms.

"Miaow," he squeaked. His eyes clouded over with pain. His breath came in little gasps.

"Pussy-willow, Pussy-willow," cried Maud, "whatever have you eaten?"

He began to writhe in agony and then, suddenly, stopped. He looked directly into her eyes, and then his body went limp.

Maud called out his name, again and again, but he didn't budge. He was dead. She held his body to her heart and rocked him, howling.

Lucy Macneill heard her granddaughter's screams and came running from the kitchen, her face white.

"Maudie, Maudie, what's happened? Are you hurt?"

Then she saw the lifeless kitten in Maud's arms. She stooped down and examined it.

"Poison," she said shortly. "He must have got into some rat poison."

Maud's sobbing grew louder.

"Oh for goodness sakes, girl," said her grandmother, "get a hold of yourself. It's only a cat!"

"He was my cat!" cried Maud. "I loved him!"

"Come now," said her grandmother, pulling the girl to her feet. "Leave him be and come and have your breakfast."

But Maud could not stop crying. Finally her grandmother sent her back to bed. At lunchtime Mrs. Macneill climbed the stairs and stood looking down at her granddaughter with her tear-streaked face.

"It's not right to mourn for an animal like that," she said. "Someday you'll have something real to grieve about, believe me. Now get up and wash your face. You're going to eat your lunch and then you're going to school, dead cat or no dead cat."

Maud did as she was told, but all afternoon she felt like a dead weight was pressing her into the ground. At recess she stood under a tree in the spruce grove and watched as the other children played. Her mouth tasted of ashes.

And yet, in the midst of her sorrow, a little part of her stood to one side, watching. That part of her saw the light filtering through the trees, noting how it created brown stripes along the trunks. That part of her marked how she felt and stored it away. That part of her would go home that night, pull out her diary, and write down everything that had happened. That part of her would rewrite the death scenes in "The Graves," using this new knowledge, and make the story even better.

Alone

Nothing about Maud Montgomery's life was easy. By the age of nine, when her kitten died in her arms, she had already experienced the loss of both parents. Her mother died when she was not quite two, and her father left her to her grandparents to bring up. He came in and out of her life, never staying long enough to make much of a difference.

Maud was an unusually sensitive child, with a quick wit and a wild imagination. She felt everything intensely, plunging from the heights of joy to the depths of despair. Her grandparents, Lucy and Alexander Macneill, were in their fifties when she came to live with them. They saw it as their duty to care for their dead daughter's child, but they found her tempestuous personality difficult. They were strict and demanding, with very clear ideas of how children should be brought up. Her grandfather had a prickly personality—he took pleasure in making cruel remarks. Her grandmother was kinder, but neither of them ever told her they loved her, or showed her any overt signs of affection. Maud learned very early that the place where she would get what she needed was not the rambling old farmhouse in Cavendish, Prince Edward Island, but in the endless realms of her imagination.

She grew up in a close-knit community, where nearly everyone was related to everyone else.

Maud's grandmother, Lucy Macneill, did her best to bring up her granddaughter, but she was baffled by the child's extreme emotions and wild imagination.

Cavendish had a school, two churches, and a post office. It was 18 kilometers (11 miles) from the nearest railway station and 39 kilometers (24 miles) from Charlottetown, the nearest city.

As a "charity child," a poor relation, and a girl to boot, Maud was not highly thought of by her many relatives. Both sides of her family were among the founding settlers of Prince Edward Island, and were now established and well respected. But Maud's father, Monty Montgomery, had a knack for starting something and then messing it up. He had been a sea captain for a while, then when he married Clara Macneill he opened up a general store—but that didn't work out. When Maud was still a toddler, Clara got very sick with tuberculosis, a lung disease, and Monty brought her home to her parents in Cavendish, where she died.

Maud was gifted with an excellent memory. All her life, she kept very clear pictures in her mind of things that happened to her as a child. Even though she was not yet two at the time, she

Maud never knew her mother, Clara Macneill Montgomery, who died when Maud was 21 months old.

remembered the day of her mother's funeral. She was wearing a white embroidered dress, the sun was shining through a green vine growing over the window, making dancing shadows on the floor, someone was crying, and her father held her tight. Her mother's face was so beautiful and peaceful that she reached out to touch her. But her skin felt cold and strange, and Maud shrank back against her father.

The little girl didn't understand, but her life was changed forever that day. With no mother, and an absent father, the child had no one to love her the way she needed to be loved. Although her grandparents loved her in their own way, they never understood her. She often felt as much an orphan as Anne of Green Gables or Emily of New Moon.

 *Echoes*

Lucy Maud Montgomery wove the experiences of her child-hood into all her books. She kept writing and rewriting her early life, as if by giving her characters happier circumstances she could somehow transform her own lonely childhood.

Three of the main characters in her most popular books were orphans or semi-orphans: Anne in Anne of Green Gables, *Emily in* Emily of New Moon, *and Sara Stanley in* The Story Girl, *who had an absentee father, just as Maud did. Anne finds an unexpectedly loving family with the stern Marilla and the eccentric Matthew. Emily finds a degree of acceptance and love with Cousin Jimmy, Aunt Laura, and Aunt Elizabeth. The Story Girl is perfectly happy living near her cousins, and then her father comes and whisks her off to Paris. They all fared better than Maud.*

The Fairy Room

Although Maud sometimes felt like an orphan, there were advantages to her situation. Lucy Macneill had a reputation as an excellent cook and housekeeper, and Maud was always well cared for physically. She had a warm winter bedroom off the living room and a summer bedroom upstairs, as well as another upstairs room for her toys. She never had to wear hand-me-down clothes or shoes. The Macneills were known for their pride, and they brought Maud up with a sense of family importance.

Lucy and Alexander Macneill had raised six children. When little Maud arrived, they still had one grown-up daughter at home, Emily. None of them was enthusiastic about an energetic two-year-old coming to live with them. Emily

Maud's bedroom at Park Corner, where she lived happily every summer with her cousins.

nagged her for being messy and making too much noise, and her grandparents were always trying to get her to behave like a grown-up.

Maud wanted to make them happy, but she couldn't help herself. She threw herself into everything she did, 100 percent. If a beautiful tree caught her eye, she would run up and hug it, then give it a name, then return to whisper secrets to it. If she was sad she was inconsolable; if happy—bursting with it.

When she was little, she felt like an alien in the house. Everyone else was grown-up. There was no one to play with. Being Maud, she didn't let this stop her. A bookcase with glass doors stood in a corner in the sitting room. Maud could see another room through the cloudy glass, one that looked much like the room she was in, but it had a misty, fairy quality. There was a little girl in the left-hand side of the bookcase, a girl who looked like Maud. Her name was Katie Maurice, and Maud had long conversations with her. They told each other secrets. In the right-hand side of the glass, Maud discovered a sad widow, Lucy Gray. In the evening, when twilight brought shadows into the corners of the room, Maud loved to go and talk to her secret friends in the glass.

Echoes

Katie Maurice appears in Anne of Green Gables, *in the door of Mrs. Thomas's bookcase. She lives in a fairyland beyond the glass, and Anne pours her heart out to her, whenever she can find time away from her chores looking after the Thomas children.*

Maud liked to play with dolls, and her father had bought her a little doll bed. She chattered away to her dolls and held tea parties, and then put them to bed. She also made friends with all the barn cats. When she started writing stories, one of her specialties was writing biographies of cats and dolls, providing them with harrowing adventures.

Borrowing a Family

One place Maud could play with children her own age was at Park Corner, where her Aunt Annie and Uncle John Campbell had a large, happy brood. They lived in a big, white farmhouse trimmed with crinkly gingerbread lattice, surrounded by a lovely old apple orchard.

Echoes

In The Story Girl, *the Kings' house and family was based on the Campbells' establishment at Park Corner. The Campbell cousins became the King children, and the tales of Judgment Day and the blue chest of Rachel Ward were true stories.*

Maud went to Park Corner every summer until she started school. The 20-kilometer (12-mile) drive took several hours by horse and buggy. The horse ambled up and down the gentle, red-ribboned road, through pretty woods and past sparkling ponds, always with a view of the sea through the trees.

Echoes

In Anne of Green Gables, *the road from Bright River to Avonlea takes much of its scenery from Maud's childhood journeys to Park Corner. When Anne drives home with Matthew from the railway station, she is transported with joy by the splendor of the countryside. She invents her own flowery names for two local beauty spots—The White Way of Delight and The Lake of Shining Waters.*

Prince Edward Island is known for its unusual red soil, caused by a high concentration of iron oxide.

At Park Corner Maud felt like she belonged to a real family, with kids running up and down stairs, shouting, laughing, always up to something. Nobody there expected children to sit quietly in a corner. There was always something delicious baking in the oven, and friends and neighbors dropped in and out. Maud and her cousins went fishing in the brook and berry-picking in the back fields. On rainy days the kids retreated to the attic, where they played dress-up.

The Cavendish Schoolhouse

When Maud was six, she started school in Cavendish at the one-room schoolhouse just across the road from her grandparents'. Perhaps the most thrilling part of this new adventure for the lonely child was the prospect of being with other children all day and making new friends.

Maud loved school. It was the first place she felt that she had some value. She had already taught herself to read, and the teacher soon realized that Maud was exceptionally bright.

The Cavendish school was known for its high standards and good teachers, and Maud's education was perfectly suited to a budding writer: careful instruction in grammar and spelling, and lots of practice writing essays, poetry, and stories.

Echoes

The schoolhouse in Anne of Green Gables *was based on the Cavendish schoolhouse. Suffering humiliations at the hands of insensitive teachers, struggling with geometry, competing with schoolmates for first place?Anne's school-days mirror Maud's experiences. Muriel Stacey is a portrait of Maud's favorite teacher, Hattie Gordon. Even the schools' surroundings are alike: the spruce wood where the Avonlea students play and eat lunch is based on the wood beside the Cavendish schoolhouse.*

When she wrote *Anne of Green Gables,* Maud based the Cuthbert farmhouse on this actual house in Cavendish. Now it is a museum.

All students were expected to learn poems by heart and then stand up and recite them. Poetry was as much a part of everyday life as popular songs are today. Maud responded passionately to the great poets from a very young age. The poetry she learned as a child stayed with her all her life.

Echoes

Anne Shirley in Anne of Green Gables *has a flair for dramatic recitals of poetry. Her enthusiasm for Alfred, Lord Tennyson's poem* Idylls of the King, *a poem about King Arthur and his court, leads Anne and her friends to act out Elaine's watery funeral.*

Maud quickly rose to the top of her class and prided herself on her good marks. The school had concerts at which all the children were encouraged to give recitations, and the story-teller in Maud loved getting up in front of an audience and holding them spellbound. She already had a reputation among her schoolmates for telling fascinating tales. She could often be seen at recess with a little group gathered around her listening to a story.

Echoes

Reciting poetry in public was part of E. B. White's education too, but unlike Lucy Maud Montgomery, he hated it.

Montgomery wrote The Story Girl *in 1910, the fourth book she completed after* Anne of Green Gables. *She always said this was her favorite. Sara Stanley is gifted with a wondrously expressive voice that captivates her listeners, both young and old.*

A World Full of Stories

Prince Edward Islanders are known for their storytelling skills. In the long winters, one of the only forms of entertainment was sitting around a wood stove spinning tales. Family stories, ghost stories, folktales from Scotland: there was an endless fund of stories to be told and retold. Grandfather Macneill had a particular talent for storytelling, and Maud could listen to him for hours. And because the Macneills ran the local post office, people were dropping in all day, often stopping to chat about the latest news. Maud liked to hide behind the door or under the table to listen to the conversations.

Good Presbyterians, the Macneills attended church at least twice on Sundays. Maud had to learn a Bible passage every week for Sunday school, and her grandfather read from the Bible every night after supper. Afterwards, Maud was allowed to read it

Echoes

The funny stories, the sad romances, and the gossip Maud heard in her childhood all made their way into her books. In The Story Girl, *"How Betty Sherman won a husband" is a Macneill family story.*

herself at the table. It was one of her favorite books: she loved the rich sound of the language, and she would repeat phrases over and over, turning the delicious words on her tongue. The colorful characters, the dramatic stories, and the resonant poetry of the Bible all worked their way into Maud's imagination and her writing.

Maud particularly loved hearing ghost stories. She relished the feeling of icy fingers crawling up her spine as the tale reached its chilling conclusion. Then she was afraid to go to bed and she hid under the covers, unable to sleep, as her imagination transformed every nighttime sound into a ghostly presence. But no matter how scared she got, the sensations of dread were so delicious that she always wanted more.

At nine years old, Maud was already writing a daily journal to express all the emotions she could not reveal to her disapproving grandparents.

 *Echoes*

Walking in Beauty

Growing up as she did, on a working farm, Maud had her own set of chores to do every day, and she learned to work hard. Not only did she have to help her grandmother in the kitchen with washing and drying dishes, preparing meals, churning butter, and making cheese, but she fed the chickens and turkeys, weeded the garden, took the cows and sheep to pasture, and during mackerel season carried three meals a day down to the men fishing by the shore. At harvest time, she gathered apples, turnips, and potatoes all day.

Maud didn't mind the outside work. Whenever she could, she raised her eyes from her task and took in the lovely scenery around her. She always noticed the view, and what the sky was doing, and how the trees were bending in the wind.

To Maud, everything around her was brimming with life and personality—from the fragrant blossom on an apple tree outside her window, to the graceful white birch at the edge of the orchard, to the gray-and-white-striped cat in the granary. She believed that when she was surrounded by the beauty of nature, she was very close to a magical world. She imagined that a thin veil was all that lay

Echoes

With its pretty farmhouses, gently rolling hills, and meandering shoreline, Prince Edward Island stirred Maud's finely tuned sense of beauty.

between her and this enchanted place, and sometimes she could see through the veil to fairyland.

> *. . . amid all the commonplaces of life, I was very near to a kingdom of ideal beauty. Between it and me hung only a thin veil. I could never draw it quite aside, but sometimes a wind fluttered it and I caught a glimpse of the enchanting realm beyond.*

Books

Apart from the Bible, Maud had access to her grandparents' bookshelves and the magazines and newspapers that made their way to Cavendish. Her reading material as a child might strike us today as a little odd: she read an assortment of adult classics and a lot of poetry, but only a few books written especially for children. One of her favorite children's authors was Hans Christian Andersen, whose fairy tales often featured lonely heroines, dramatic self-sacrifice, and heartbreaking endings. All these elements appealed to Maud's sense of what made a good story.

As she grew older, Maud discovered that there was indeed a fairyland beyond the glass doors of the bookcase in the living room—the books she found there transported her to magnificent, far-off places. She particularly enjoyed Charles Dickens' London in *The Pickwick Papers* and the Scottish highlands in Sir Walter Scott's adventure story *Rob Roy*. In her imagination she walked the streets of Naples, Italy, as described in the strange love story *Zanoni*, by Edward Bulwer-Lytton. These books were written for adults and not really suitable for children, but Maud didn't care: the romance, the exotic locations, and the characters fed her ever-hungry imagination.

With her characteristic passion, Maud memorized whole chapters of books she loved so she could pretend that she was living inside them. On Sundays, religious books were the only kind of book Maud was allowed to read. She was enthralled by *The Memoir of Anzonetta Peters,* about an unlikely little girl of five who became deathly ill and decided to be saintly for the few years left to her. She did good deeds constantly and spoke in quotations from hymns. She lasted until the age of twelve, when she succumbed to her illness. The drama and the tragedy of her situation caught Maud's imagination, and for a while she tried to live as much as possible like this holy little girl. Wisely, she decided not to try to speak in hymns.

One of the main sources of Maud's reading material came every month in the form of women's magazines. Her favorite was *Godey's Lady's Book,* which was filled with the latest fashions, short stories, and serial novels. She enjoyed them all, whether they were romantic, silly, sentimental, touching, or melodramatic.

Maud didn't have access to a public library to get new books, so she borrowed books from adults whenever she had the chance.

The Weirdest Kid

Hans Christian Andersen
1805–1875

Of all the weird little kids in the history of the world, Hans Christian Andersen was definitely one of the weirdest. Tall and gangly, always growing out of his threadbare clothes, he wandered the streets of Odense, Denmark, with his eyes closed, imagining himself into a fairy story. He wrote poems, songs, and stories and read and sang them to everyone he met, informing them that he was a genius and destined for greatness.

Rather than spend his time with other children, Hans Christian preferred to play with his toy theater, making clothes for his puppets and dolls. He was a frequent visitor to the local insane asylum, where he and the inmates exchanged stories. When threatened by rough boys, he sang to them to stop them from beating him up.

Hans Christian never doubted that he was born for better things than the tiny house where he lived with his shoemaker father and washerwoman mother. Although they were desperately poor, his father shared his love of books and reading with his son, while his mother entertained him with folktales. Because they couldn't afford to buy books, Hans Christian wheedled his way into richer people's houses and asked to borrow their books, taking the opportunity to read them his stories and sing a few songs. He never doubted that the whole world wanted to hear him, even when other children or even teachers picked on him.

Tragedy struck when he was 11: his father died, and Hans Christian had to go to work in a factory to help put food on the table. The bullying and the harsh working conditions were too much for him and he didn't last long at any job. When he was 14 he set off with a bundle of clothes to make his fortune in Copenhagen, the capital of Denmark. He was determined to perform at the Royal Theatre, and he kept trying until the theatre company gave him a chance. He was so funny-looking that his first stage role was as a troll.

Through the kind sponsorship of friends, Hans Christian eventually managed to get an education and when he was 30, he wrote his first book of fairy tales. Using the rich source of traditional tales he'd heard from his mother, as well as the classical stories he knew so well, he created new fairy tales that seemed very old. He became famous. Both children and adults immediately responded to his poignant, often funny, and wildly imaginative stories such as "The Emperor's New Clothes" and "The Ugly Duckling." Many of his stories seem to be about himself and the way he reacted to the world. Despite his fame, he always felt like an outsider looking in on other people's happiness, the poor little weird kid who would never really belong anywhere.

Hans Christian Andersen wrote more than 150 fairy tales. Among the most well known are "The Little Mermaid," "The Red Shoes," "Thumbelina," "The Princess and the Pea," "The Nightingale," "The Snow Queen," and "The Little Matchgirl."

When she was 13, a literary society was formed in Cavendish. This brought a lending library, visiting speakers, and discussion groups into the small community. It opened up a larger world of writers, ideas, and books to the girl who had been writing in secret for years.

Writing It Out

"I cannot remember the time when I was not writing, or when I did not mean to be an author. To write has always been my central purpose around which every hope and effort and ambition of my life has grouped itself."

Much as she had turned to her imaginary friends in the glass doors of the bookcase when she was little, as she grew up Maud turned to writing to satisfy her need for companionship. Her grandparents did not encourage her to express her strange ideas and fancies about the world, so she bottled them up inside and then wrote them out in her journal.

Maud's lifelong habit of keeping a daily journal began when she was nine. In it she recorded her daily activities, her feelings, her thoughts, her dreams. Paper was scarce in those days, but for once her disagreeable grandfather helped her out.

He came from a family where writing was respected, and he was a good writer himself. He let her have the letter bills that came to the post office—long sheets of paper that were printed on only one side. She used these for her stories and poems. A medical company sent out little yellow notebooks as an advertising gimmick, and her grandfather let her have those too, for her journals.

Echoes

In Emily of New Moon, *Aunt Laura gives Emily Starr a stack of letter bills to write on, just like the ones Maud obtained from her grandfather. Emily squirrels them away like precious treasure and uses them to write letters to her dead father. She recounts her daily activities and expresses her deepest feelings in these letters, just as Maud did in her journals. Her hiding place for her writing is the same as Maud's: inside a sofa frame.*

Maud hoarded pencil stubs and spent every spare moment writing in her journal or composing stories. Her stories were wildly dramatic; many of her characters met untimely deaths by execution, shipwreck, pirates, and fatal diseases. Like her characters Anne and Emily, she loved using new words—the bigger the better. She started experimenting with poetry, and one day she summoned the courage to show her visiting father a poem she had written. It was in blank verse (which means it didn't rhyme), in imitation of a poem she admired. Her father dismissed it with a laugh, saying it didn't sound like poetry.

Maud was mortified. She destroyed the poem and started hiding her writing away in a secret place inside the sofa frame, vowing never to show her work to anyone again. However, she was not one to give up. She continued to write poetry and stories, and, of course, long entries in her journal. Whatever happened to upset her during the day was written out in the journal at night. There, her stormy feelings found understanding and relief. Her journal became her best friend.

Lucy Maud Montgomery, E. B. White, C. S. Lewis, Madeleine L'Engle, and Philip Pullman all wrote poetry while they were growing up.

A Turbulent Teenager

As she grew into a teenager, Maud was often in need of the solace provided by her journal. Her grandparents retreated from the society around them, seldom having visitors and discouraging

Maud from bringing friends home. Maud was itching to participate in all the local social activities—sleigh rides, skating parties, church events, and picnics. Her grandparents allowed her to do some of these, but as she grew more restless and demanding, they tightened their grip.

By now, Maud was growing into a vivacious, popular young woman, with lots of friends and several boys who admired her. She was always near the top of her class with her schoolwork, and her writing skills were developing. But in her heart, there was still that longing that had been with her ever since her mother's death: she wanted to belong to a family circle with a mother and father who loved her. When her father remarried, and set up house in Prince Albert, Saskatchewan, it seemed like maybe her dream could come true. A plan was hatched that she would travel out west by rail with her grandfather Montgomery and settle down with her father, his wife, and their two-year-old daughter.

Echoes

Emily of New Moon was published in 1923, when Montgomery was 49. She said that this character was the closest to her own. An orphan, Emily lives with the Murrays, who, like the Macneills, are known for their pride. Stern Aunt Elizabeth is closely modeled on Grandmother Macneill, and Emily decides at a very young age that she will be a writer. The book explores the passion that drives a writer like Montgomery to transform her experience into words. Emily's need to write every day is just as strong as her need to eat.

A Wicked Stepmother

Maud was 15 when she left Cavendish to make the 4,000-kilometer (2,500-mile) train trip to Saskatchewan with her grandfather,

An infrequent visitor, Hugh John Montgomery could be charming and affectionate, but he was never there when Maud really needed him.

Senator Donald Montgomery. The trans-Canada railway had just been completed five years before, in 1885. Maud, for whom a trip to Charlottetown 39 kilometers (24 miles) away was a marvelous treat, found rail travel both exciting and exhausting. In Regina, she was reunited with her father, whom she hadn't seen since she was nine. They had an affectionate and tearful reunion and then they continued the trip to Prince Albert.

In contrast to the settled farmland of Prince Edward Island, Maud's new home was a rough frontier town along the North Saskatchewan River. Maud's hopes of a loving family circle faded away in the first week. Her new stepmother, Mary Ann, was only about eight years older than Maud. She resented this bright, lively young girl, and the affection her husband so obviously felt for her. She did everything she could to make

Maud feel unwanted: she made snide comments about her hair and her clothes and told her husband to stop calling his daughter "Maudie" because it was too childish. She also read Maud's private letters. Maud tried to hide how much her stepmother hurt her feelings. She didn't want to upset her father.

When Mary Ann had a new baby, she kept Maud home from school to look after the children and do the housework. Her father, not wanting to rock the boat, said nothing, and Maud gritted her teeth and became a Cinderella, slaving all day while her stepmother made social calls.

 ## Echoes

Montgomery used her experience working for her stepmother as a starting point for her descriptions of Anne's early years of drudgery. While Maud had just two small children to care for, poor Anne has to deal first with Mrs. Thomas's four youngsters and then with Mrs. Hammond's three sets of twins.

Although Maud made some good friends and had an active social life in Prince Albert, she didn't want to go on living as an unpaid servant. She had been homesick for her beloved Cavendish ever since she stepped off the train, so after a year away she returned to Prince Edward Island.

Recognition at Last

Even though the year in Prince Albert was difficult for Maud, she accomplished something during that time that she had been striving towards for years: three of her poems were published in newspapers. She was on her way: a published writer at the age of 16.

When she arrived at her grandparents' home in Cavendish, she threw dignity aside and ran around hugging everyone,

When this picture was taken, Maud was 28. She was living quietly in Cavendish, looking after her grandmother and writing stories in her spare time.

including animals and trees, expressing her delight at being home at last. Prince Edward Island would always be home for Maud Montgomery. Whatever unhappiness she experienced there, the island had captured her soul, never to let go. In later years, when she moved away for good, she kept it alive inside her and wrote about it again and again in her books.

Grown-up Life

With her excellent marks, if Maud had been a boy she would have been sent to college and even university as a matter of course. But in those days, most people believed that education was wasted on girls, who were encouraged to get married and have children instead.

Grandfather Macneill was set against any more schooling

for Maud, and he refused to contribute any money. But Grandmother Macneill decided that Maud should have more education, and she offered some of her own money and persuaded Maud's father to contribute. Maud placed fifth in the province in the Prince of Wales College entrance exams, and moved to Charlottetown to train as a schoolteacher. Like Anne, she crammed two years of study into one so she could get out into the world sooner. Despite the fact that her grouchy grandfather refused to lend her the horse to go to interviews, she got a job.

Maud taught school in a small town, boarding with a minister's family. She saved her money carefully and at the end of the year, with help from her grandmother, she had enough to finance a year at Dalhousie University in Halifax. She did very well, but her money ran out and the following fall she returned to teaching.

Maud taught in one-room schools, like the one in Cavendish. The work was demanding, but she rose early to write before school started, often wrapping herself in quilts to keep warm. By now, she was regularly getting stories and poems published in magazines in Canada and the United States. She was more determined than ever to make writing her full-time career.

Her plans took an unexpected turn when her grandfather Macneill died suddenly when she was 24. Maud gave up teaching and went home to look after her grandmother. For the next 13 years, Maud lived in the farmhouse with her grandmother, running the household and the post office, and writing—always writing. She never saw her father again; he died in Alberta when she was 26. Most of her friends had moved away from Cavendish, into the bigger world, and she was very lonely.

Leaving the Island

One day in 1906, Maud was looking for an idea for a story and she found a note in her workbook about an orphan girl who came to a family who had wanted a boy. It captured her imagination and she started her story. It took her two years to finish writing it and find a publisher who was interested, but by June 20, 1908, she held her first book in her hands.

Anne of Green Gables was a runaway bestseller, and its popularity pushed Maud into the limelight. She made a lot of money, but her grandmother wouldn't let her spend any of it on improvements to the house. Lucy Macneill became rather queer as she aged, refusing to heat the house properly or have visitors. Maud suffered through it, writing her books on her desk by the window in her little room upstairs, or by the kitchen fire in the winter. She knew this situation wouldn't last forever.

A cozy reading corner in Maud's room in the Cavendish farmhouse.

About the time she started writing *Anne,* Maud became secretly engaged to the local minister, Ewan Macdonald. Although she wasn't madly in love with him, she liked him a lot, and she longed to be a married woman, with children.

Just four short months after her grandmother died, Maud married Ewan at Park Corner. They moved to a parish in Leaksdale, Ontario. She would never again live in her treasured Prince Edward Island.

The Thin Veil

Maud led a very full life, bringing up two sons, meeting the many demands of being a minister's wife, running a house, and writing book after book. She was celebrated around the world for her children's novels, but in private she still poured all her troubles and frustrations into her journal. She was beset with family worries, legal battles, and illness.

In Montgomery's books, nearly all set in an idyllically beautiful Prince Edward Island, her heroines struggle through difficulties but usually grow up to marry for love, with happy families. This wasn't Maud's own life. She had to leave her beloved island, she married for convenience, and her family was chronically unhappy. Although she became one of the most famous Canadian writers, and her charming stories have captured the imaginations of millions of children, she suffered real tragedy in her own life.

Maud died of a drug overdose in 1942, at the age of 68. It's a very sad ending to the story of the imaginative child who took such delight in the natural world, and felt everything so deeply.

In her books, Maud created the world the way she wanted it to be. In her life she didn't have that kind of control. But after 100 years, readers around the world continue to laugh and cry along with Anne, Emily, and all her other vivid characters as they struggle to grow up in the mirror world that is so like our own,

Maud always considered Prince Edward Island her true home. She was buried there.

and yet so enchantingly different. Her books give us the glimpse she had of the elusive beauty hidden behind the thin veil that separates our world from the world of the imagination.

BOOKS

Montgomery wrote 20 novels and several other books of collected stories and poetry. The ones listed below are the most popular.

Anne of Green Gables
Anne of Avonlea
Anne of the Island
Anne's House of Dreams
The Story Girl
Emily of New Moon
Emily Climbs
Emily's Quest

Maud's House of Dreams, by Janet Lunn, is an excellent biography of Lucy Maud Montgomery.

power of your imagination

If you love reading books, you know what it is like to lose yourself in a story. Your bedroom drops away and you're in the world of the book, side by side with the hero or heroine. Your ticket to those other worlds depends on the power of your imagination and the power of the words you're reading. The best writers scoop you up and take you on a ride that only ends on the last page of the book.

To create this kind of magic, a writer needs a very special kind of imagination.

Clive Staples Lewis
(1898–1963)

Sea and Islands

Writer

What happens to people makes who they are.

To create this kind of magic, a writer needs a very special kind of imagination.

*J*ack gazed out the small attic window. It was raining. Just like yesterday, and the day before, and the day before that. He could just make out the long, dark line of hills on the horizon. A faint glow from the sky beyond set them shimmering with a silvery light—perhaps the sun was trying to break through in the west.

Jack looked down at the notebook open on the table in front of him. Lord Big, a huge frog dressed in tails and top hat, had just given a rousing speech to the government of Boxen, urging them to build a new railway. Bunny and Hawki, the two young princes, were running wild as usual and Lord Big had to leave Parliament to scold them for their shenanigans. Meanwhile, there was a plot under way to oust Lord Big from his leadership role and ongoing skirmishes on the borders between the Mouse Knights and the dangerous Cats.

The boy sighed and put down his pen. He didn't really feel like writing today. He had a toothache, and his head hurt. The

house was full of strange rumblings and footsteps. He should carry on with the Boxen story so that later tonight he could write to his brother and tell him all the latest delicious developments. Warnie was away at school in England and Jack missed him.

The wall above the makeshift table was completely covered with drawings and maps of Boxen and the people who lived there. Jack's part of Boxen was Animal-Land, where animals dressed up like humans. Warnie's territory was India, crisscrossed by his beloved railways. Ships with tall masts plowed the seas around Boxen, every detail of the masts and rigging carefully rendered.

Around him, the room was in its usual state of lovely mess. Stacks of papers, books, drawings, and notebooks spilled off the desk and onto the floor. Old toys lay forgotten in the corner. A layer of dust coated everything Jack hadn't touched in the last few days.

Jack got up from the desk and walked over to open a small door in the far wall. Even though he was only nine, he had to stoop to go through it. This next room was empty except for a couple of old trunks that stood against the wall, waiting for the next visit to the seaside when they would be hauled down and filled with clothes, pails, shovels, and books. Jack crossed to an even smaller door under the sloping ceiling, dropped to his knees, and crawled into the darkness. A kind of tunnel ran along the length of the house, outside the regular walls of the rooms. Jack knew his way even without a flashlight, for this was one of *his favorite places. When he felt a softness brush his fingers, he stopped and curled up on the blanket that lay there.*

He held his right hand against the sore side of his face and listened. He was right up under the roof tiles. The wind whistled mournfully, edging in wherever there was a broken brick or a hole under a windowsill. Rainwater gushed through the eavestroughs, and water cisterns gurgled a few rooms away. Jack could also hear a faraway murmuring of voices: maids, nurses, doctors. His father. And under it all he thought he could hear his mother crying, the way he'd been hearing her every night for the longest time.

Jack's mother was sick. And she wasn't getting better.

Parents Who Ran Hot and Cold

When C. S. Lewis was four years old, he walked up to his mother one day and pointed at his chest. "He is Jacksie," he said firmly. He didn't like his real name (Clive), so he decided to give himself a new one. From then on he was Jacksie to everyone, and as he grew older it was shortened to Jack.

Jack and his older brother, Warnie, were best friends as well as brothers—they didn't often play with other children. When they were little, they were taught at home by either a governess or their mother. Although three years younger, quick-witted Jack was the chief instigator of many of their boyhood adventures. Once, enchanted by the Irish fairy tales told by Lizzie, their nursemaid, Jack decided that the leprechaun's legendary pot of gold was buried at the end of a rainbow in their garden. The two boys eagerly began to dig up the front path. When they were called away to tea, they forgot all about it and their father fell into it on his way home from work. Furious, he refused to believe in Jack's pot-of-gold story. He thought his sons had dug the hole deliberately to play a trick on him.

Jack and Warnie found it difficult to trust their father. One day he'd be affectionate and funny, spinning tales and helping Jack with his writing. The next he'd be gloomy and worried about money, telling them they would all end up in the work-house (a dreadful kind of jail that homeless people had to live in). Albert Lewis had a vile temper and would lose it at the drop of a hat. But when he was feeling happy, he would scoop the boys up and whisk them down to the Belfast harbor to watch the ships come in. Albert was a lawyer, an excellent speaker (he wanted to be a politician but it never worked out), and a born worrier. His emotions went up and down like a jack-in-the-box.

Jack's mother, Flora Lewis, was an altogether different cup of tea. Calm, cool, and collected, she studied mathematics and

This ruined archway in the Irish Mourne Mountains echoes the door to nowhere at the end of *Prince Caspian*.

logic at university. She and Albert were childhood friends, and Albert was madly in love with her for a long time. But she wasn't at all sure she loved him enough to marry him, so she held back for several years and didn't give in to his passionate pleas until she was 32. Cheerful and steady, she became the calm center of the family, and Albert adored her.

Books Everywhere

One thing Albert and Flora shared was their love of books. They bought books all the time and read constantly. After supper, they each liked nothing better than to curl up in an armchair and read until it was time to go to bed. Surrounded by books, Jack quickly learned to read and then set out on what was to be his life's greatest adventure: reading everything he could get his hands on.

There were books in the study, books in the drawing room, books in the cloakroom, books (two deep) in the great bookcase on the landing, books in a bedroom, books piled as high as my shoulder in the cistern attic... In the seemingly endless rainy afternoons I took volume after volume from the shelves.

One of Jack's favorite authors when he was small was Beatrix Potter, whose little books featured animals dressed like humans down to the smallest detail. They inspired him to start drawing animals wearing clothes. Then he began to make up stories about them, starting with his toy rabbit, Bunny. Bunny soon became the king of an imaginary country called Animal-Land. As time went by, the make-believe world grew ever more complicated and detailed.

When Jack was eight, he developed an intense interest in medieval times. In *The Strand Magazine*, he read *Sir Nigel*, by Arthur Conan Doyle (author of the Sherlock Holmes stories), which appeared every month in installments. This was an ongoing tale of a brave hero in the fourteenth century who embarked on a series of adventures marked by jousts, intrigues, battles, and near-death injuries. He is finally awarded a knighthood for his valor. As Jack fell deeper under the spell of medieval romance, Animal-Land took on a distinctly medieval flavor and Sir Peter Mouse, a gallant knight, sprang to life to take on the fearsome struggle against the Cats.

Echoes

Although Lewis insisted that Animal-Land was not an earlier version of Narnia, it is hard not to see some similarities. Animals that talk inhabit both countries, and in Narnia the medieval influence is strong. Characters often talk, dress, and behave as if they stepped out of a medieval tale. Reepicheep and Sir Peter Mouse have much in common: the most noble of mice, Reepicheep displays all the flourish of a classic knight with a finely tuned sense of honor and a fierce courage far beyond his size.

Jack discovered another author in *The Strand* who quickly became a favorite: E. Nesbit. He enjoyed her engaging stories about kids who continually got into trouble without meaning to. Some of her books involved time travel and magic. C. S. Lewis loved them so much that, when he was in his twenties, he had a wonderful dream about finding a new Nesbit story in a railway station. In the dream, he was so excited about reading the story that he missed his train.

Both Madeleine L'Engle and C. S. Lewis loved E. Nesbit's books.

After listening to the Irish folktales and legends told by his nursemaid, Lizzie, Jack developed an appetite for fairy tales and myths that lasted all his life. But his reading went far beyond children's books: by the time he was 10 he had read several of Shakespeare's plays as well as *Paradise Lost*, a book-length poem about heaven and hell by John Milton.

The books Jack loved as a child nurtured his vivid imagination. As he read, he could see pictures in his head that were often more real to him than the objects around him. But the rambling house he grew up in also played a major role in shaping his imagination, and certain aspects of it made their way into his Narnia books.

Jack loved the rugged Mourne Mountains, not far from his home in Belfast, and he thought of them when he created Narnia.

Dirty Daisy

Edith Nesbit
1858–1924

Children have enjoyed the books written by E. Nesbit for nearly 100 years. She wrote about ordinary children in Victorian England who played imaginative games that inevitably landed them in trouble. Some of her books involved magic and time travel. Nesbit created likable, believable characters who had wonderful adventures.

Edith Nesbit, known as Daisy when she was young, experienced a topsy-turvy childhood with blissful highs and quite wretched lows. Her father died when she was only four, and she carried the sadness of his death with her all through her life. She had two older sisters and two older brothers. One of her sisters, Mary, suffered from tuberculosis (a lung disease), and her mother carted the children around Europe and England, trying to find a place with healthy air that would make Mary better.

Daisy was shunted in and out of several boarding schools. During the holidays, she ran wild with her brothers. Many of her books are based on their shenanigans. Daisy became something of a tomboy, but she was tormented by a vivid imagination that inspired both nightmares and obsessive daytime fears.

While she was with her family, Daisy was usually happy, but she had many trying experiences at boarding schools. At one school, meals were taken away as a punishment. With messy hair, disheveled clothes, and dirty hands (as well as difficulties with math), Daisy found herself without lunch or dinner every couple of days. She spent long, hungry hours in empty classrooms and cried herself to sleep at night. She tried to escape from the school by climbing out the window and running away, but hunger drove her back.

Mary died when Daisy was 13. The family moved back to England and settled down in a country house that Nesbit later used as the setting for *The Railway Children*. Daisy started writing poetry when she was a teenager, and it was published in magazines. She continued her writing career with novels, plays, magazine articles, and ghost stories, and finally came to writing children's stories in middle age. She wrote more than 40 books for children, and they have remained popular.

Her best-known books are *The Story of the Treasure Seekers*, *The Wouldbegoods*, *The Phoenix and the Carpet*, *The Story of the Amulet*, and *The Railway Children*.

The Lewis family and friends on the front steps of Little Lea. Warnie is leaning against the pillar, with Jack beside him. Flora stands at the right in the back row, and Albert is holding the dog.

The Little End Room

When Jack was seven, his family moved to Little Lea, a brand-new house designed by his father in the suburbs of Belfast. The large three-story house had big bay windows, several chimneys, and lots of wasted space that resulted in interesting nooks and crannies for boys to play in. Jack and Warnie took over the attic: tucked under the roof, a series of small rooms led into each other through little doors. There was even a way to get into a tunnel that ran outside the proper walls.

The "little end room" became the boys' private retreat: they set up a study for themselves and spent many blissful hours there talking, reading, writing stories, and drawing pictures. Parents and maids never came in to tidy up or interfere. Because it rained a lot in Belfast and their parents had strict rules about not going out in wet weather, Warnie and Jack had many long afternoons to fill when their lessons were done. They developed the closest kind of relationship: it was Jack and Warnie together against the world.

Echoes

When Lewis wrote The Magician's Nephew, *he drew inspiration from the wonderful attic at Little Lea. The adventures begin in the dusty old tunnel that runs along under the eaves of a row of attached houses. Polly makes a hideout for herself in one corner and spends hours up there writing a story and drinking ginger beer. Later she and Digory explore the tunnel further and they discover Uncle Andrew's study. Magic rings, guinea pigs, and the unscrupulous plots of an evil magician soon follow.*

The same year they moved to Little Lea, Warnie went off to boarding school in England, so Jack was left behind to count the days till his brother's return. He spent more time with his mother. She taught him French, Latin, and math in the morning. If the weather was dry, they would go for walks in the countryside in the afternoon. Little Lea was in a new suburb, surrounded by the most glorious Irish landscape: meadows, little woods, hills, and mountains in the distance. When Warnie was home, he and Jack loved to go exploring on their bikes.

Adrift

Flora Lewis died from cancer when Jack was nine. Just two weeks after her death, Jack Lewis stood on a railway platform in Belfast watching his father cry. The brokenhearted Albert Lewis was sending Jack to school in England with his brother Warnie. He didn't want to say goodbye to his sons, but he thought it was the right thing to do. In those days, packing your children off to boarding school was considered the best way to educate them.

Echoes

Lewis said that the Narnian countryside was inspired by the Ireland of his childhood. The majestic Mourne Mountains, visible from Belfast, the seacoast at Antrim, and the hills and meadows of County Down all came to life as the wild and lovely Narnian landscape.

> *With my mother's death all settled happiness ... disappeared from my life. There was to be much fun, many pleasures, many stabs of Joy; but no more of the old security. It was sea and islands now; the great continent had sunk like Atlantis.*

All the contentment of Jack's life fell away. He suffered two shocks: he lost his mother and then he was wrenched away from everything that was familiar. For months he prayed that she would come back and his life would return to normal.

Echoes

In The Magician's Nephew, *the first time we meet Digory he has been crying in the back garden because his mother is dying. Later in the story he thinks he might be able to cure her by getting her an apple from the Tree of Life in the newly created world of Narnia. Lewis writes passionately about Digory's anguish over his mother's illness, and his desperate hope that a miracle might save her.*

The School Run by a Madman

If Jack had been sent to a normal English boarding school, the adjustment would have been bad enough. But somehow his hapless father chose one of the nastiest schools in England. Wynyard School was a desolate little place with only a handful of pupils. It had no playing fields, library, or proper teachers. The boys were taught very little: most of the time they had to sit doing the same math problems over and over again. The food was disgusting and the only bathroom was a stinking outhouse.

The very worst thing about Wynyard School was

Boarding School Blues

In England and Ireland when Jack Lewis was growing up, it was the custom for middle-class families to send their kids to boarding school from about the age of eight. Very few parents questioned the tradition: it was considered the best way for children to be educated. They slept, ate, played, and studied with other children and went home to their parents during the holidays.

People in those days didn't think children needed their parents to be as involved in their lives as parents are today. They believed that children would learn independence at boarding school. The rough-and-tumble life was considered a good preparation for the big, bad world.

Unfortunately, although some of the schools were good, many weren't. In boys' schools particularly, a system of self-rule developed. The older boys could use the younger ones as unpaid servants, and often made life miserable for them.

If you were slow at your lessons, cheeky to teachers, late, or misbehaved in any way, you might find yourself on the receiving end of a beating. Teachers regularly punished students by hitting them with a wooden cane. Today, a teacher who hits a student will quickly find themselves in big trouble, but when Jack Lewis was a boy, corporal punishment was an accepted part of boarding school. So was lack of privacy and homesickness.

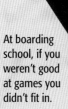

At boarding school, if you weren't good at games you didn't fit in.

that it was run by a madman. Brutal and bad tempered, Rev. Robert Capron (known as "Oldie" to the students) found great delight in bullying and beating boys. He beat children for making mistakes. He beat them if they were from a poor family. And he beat them if he just didn't like the look of

C. S. Lewis and Madeleine L'Engle both wrote letters home pleading to be released from boarding schools they hated.

them. All the other students had to watch his violent attacks on their friends. Jack and Warnie wrote many letters begging their father to take them out of the horrible place. Albert responded slowly, asking a relative to look into the conditions at the school and leaving his boys to struggle through the experience as best they could.

For the first time, Jack started paying attention in church, listening carefully to the Bible readings and the sermons. He began to pray fervently and grew fearful that if he didn't live up to the high Christian ideals, he would go to hell. Night after night he lay awake in the freezing dormitory, staring out the curtainless windows at the moon, imagining what it would be like to burn for eternity in hellfire. On the long walks that took the place of games, he talked to other boys about what they believed about God. The one saving grace at Wynyard was the way the students banded together in the face of Oldie's brutality. Jack found some comfort in the friendship of the other boys.

Lord Big Rules the Roost

Jack and Warnie lived for the holidays, when they would make the journey back to Ireland together. While Albert Lewis was at work, they were free to play outside or retreat to the little room in the attic and the ongoing saga of Boxen. They got a big kick out of writing their father into their stories as Lord Big, a pompous but passionate frog who gave eloquent speeches, fought duels, lost his

Jack (left) and Warnie (right) made the most of their school holidays, going on long bike rides in the beautiful Irish countryside.

temper, and was always telling the two princes (Bunny and Hawki) to wear warm clothes and go to bed on time.

C. S. Lewis, Lucy Maud Montgomery, Madeleine L'Engle, and Philip Pullman all had difficulties with their fathers—who were dead, dying, distant, or hard to get along with.

When Albert came home, he expected them to spend every minute with him. He dominated the conversation and didn't listen properly when they talked to him. The boys dreaded the time they were forced to be with their father.

Albert had grown very distraught after his wife died. His father and one of his brothers died within the same year. Already excitable, he nearly cracked under the strain. He flew into rages easily and yelled at his sons. Then he dissolved in tears. They drew back, appalled by his violent displays of emotion. They needed some sense of ongoing security, but that had disappeared with their mother. Albert loved them but he didn't know how to reach them, and everything he did pushed them farther away. They had only each other to depend on. Sadly, as they grew up, they disliked their father more and more.

Reprieve

Jack's two-year ordeal at Wynyard finally came to an end when the school closed due to lack of pupils. A year later, Rev. Robert Capron was committed to an insane asylum. Jack found himself back in Belfast, boarding at a much better school, Campbell College. After a few weeks, he developed a bad cold in his chest and his father took him out of school. For the next two months, Jack was in heaven: home alone most of the time, he spent hours and hours reading fairy tales.

After Christmas, it all came to an end and he was shipped off to another English boarding school, this time on his own; Warnie had advanced to a high school called Malvern College. Jack, aged 11, was at middle-school level, so he went to Cherbourg Preparatory School, in Great Malvern, the same town where Warnie was at school.

 Echoes

Most of the children in The Chronicles of Narnia *go to boarding schools.* In The Lion, the Witch and the Wardrobe, *Edmund's boarding school is blamed for some of his ugly behavior. And Eustace Scrubb and Jill Pole attend an experimental boarding school in* The Silver Chair, *where they are tormented by a gang of student bullies.*

The boys' favorite part of going to school in England was the railway journeys back and forth to Ireland in the holidays. They figured out how to make the most of the stopovers in Liverpool so they could eat at a restaurant and take in a show at a music hall before they caught the boat home. Warnie introduced Jack to smoking cigarettes when he was 12, and they both considered themselves very cool indeed.

Echoes

Prince Caspian begins with the four Pevensie children on a railway platform waiting for their trains to school. They've made part of the journey together, and now they must separate as the girls go in one direction for their school and the boys head off in the other. The first part of their trip still seemed like the holidays, but now they are all a bit glum as they realize that the holidays are really over and they will be stuck in school again.

Jack did well at Cherbourg. He delved into his studies with energy, and it was soon evident that he was a remarkably bright and gifted student. He entertained the other boys with stories, teased the teachers, and felt quite at home. But inside Jack, profound changes were taking place.

Joy and the North

Jack Lewis stopped believing in God when he was 12. As he studied Greek and Roman myths, he began to question why the Christian god should be any more real than the ancient gods that no one believed in anymore. After torturing himself about what was the right way to pray and living with vivid images of everlasting damnation, it was a relief to give it all up.

Something else had been stirring in Jack for a long time, something far removed from the dry Anglican church services and guilt-ridden prayers. Since he was a little boy he had experienced moments of intense joy, a mixture of memory and longing that pierced him to the heart. The first time he felt it, he was standing by a beautiful flowering bush and he suddenly remembered a little toy garden his brother had created and brought into his nursery. Jack responded passionately to beauty in nature, and he found himself yearning to experience the sense of joy again.

When Jack was 11, he found joy in a totally unexpected place. Arthur Rackham, a popular illustrator of children's books, had drawn a compelling portrait of Siegfried, the hero of Norse myths. The beauty of this picture so fired Jack's imagination that he read everything he could about Northern European mythology. He discovered that the German composer Richard Wagner had based a series of operas on Siegfried's story, called *The Ring of the Nibelung*. Jack immersed himself in the music. A vision of the North drew him in and held him fast. He was captivated by the wild romance of the cold, remote landscape where gods and humans battled under vast skies. He was growing out of the world of Boxen, and his head was filling with the gods and heroes of the North.

Life by the Bell

With his acceptance at Malvern College, Jack began a time of his life when the contrast between his inner and outer worlds was at its most extreme. While his imagination soared in a cold Northern otherworld with Siegfried and his lover Brunhilde, in the real world he was stuck in the narrow confines of a British public school.

From the first bell of the day that woke him up until the one at night that signaled lights out, Jack was on the run. Every minute of the day was scheduled: classes, chapel, sports (which he hated). He had 45 minutes more or less free in the morning, which he was supposed to use to prepare translations, but he usually spent that time polishing shoes or running errands for older boys.

British boarding schools were run on traditional principles. Everything was about fitting in. The popular boys—the good athletes—ruled the school. Older boys made the younger

Arthur Rackham's illustration of Siegfried setting off on his adventures, leaving Brunhilde behind.

ones do all kinds of chores for them. The more they disliked a boy, the more they asked him to do. Jack was cheeky and rebellious, and he had a sense of superiority he could not hide. He was smarter and better read than nearly everybody there, but that just made him irritating to the other boys, not popular.

These gas lamps illuminate the paths of a park in Great Malvern, where Jack went to school. They are said to be the inspiration for the lamppost in *The Lion, the Witch and the Wardrobe*.

They would take one look at his expression and set him a list of things to do. Behind their backs he made fun of them and gave them silly nicknames, but he had to do as he was told or risk beatings and even more chores.

As a result, he was exhausted all the time. Trying to keep up with the heavy workload as he stumbled from class to playing field to chapel, with his spare time eaten up by the whims of the older boys he despised, he was soon bone tired and desperate. The only refuge was the library, where no one was allowed to give him chores. But he couldn't get there anywhere near as often as he wanted to. He wrote a series of letters to his father, pleading to be taken out of the school.

The Great Knock

Albert Lewis finally gave in to Jack's entreaties and sent him to study with his old headmaster, William T. Kirkpatrick (known as "The Great Knock"), who tutored boys privately. Jack spent two years living with this whiskery, eccentric teacher in a small town in England, undertaking a wide course of reading in Greek, Latin, Italian, French, and German. Hungry for knowledge, he had at last found the place and the person that would make it possible for him to immerse himself completely in the life of the mind.

Echoes

Professor Kirke in The Lion, the Witch and the Wardrobe *was inspired by The Great Knock. His gruff manner, his somewhat wild appearance, his insistence upon logical thinking, and even his name were all borrowed from Jack's tutor.*

Grown-up Life

Jack passed his entrance exams and won a scholarship to Oxford University when he was 18, but he was only to spend a few weeks there before enlisting in the army and going to fight in France in the First World War. He was wounded, but he recovered. After the war he returned to Oxford, where he stayed for most of his adult life. He graduated with first-class honors and went on to be a professor of English. Although he is best known for his children's fantasy books, he also wrote science fiction and books about literature and Christianity.

Jack Lewis and J. R. R. Tolkien met with friends every Tuesday night at the Eagle and Child pub in Oxford, discussing the books they were writing.

C. S. Lewis came back to believing in God when he was in his early thirties. There was a battle waging inside him for many years. While his logical mind told him God could not exist, his mystical experiences of "joy" told a much different story. Many of his best friends at Oxford were Christians, including J. R. R. Tolkien (who wrote *The Hobbit* and *The Lord of the Rings*). Through a combination of reading books by Christian thinkers and engaging in lengthy discussions with his friends, along with his growing conviction that he could feel the presence of God all around him, Lewis was reluctantly converted.

Once Jack believed in God, he started writing books and talking on the radio about his conversion, his beliefs, and the meaning of Christianity.

A Faun in a Forest

When Jack was about 16, he kept seeing a faun in his mind—a faun in a wintery forest carrying parcels and holding an umbrella. This image recurred over the years. During the Second World War, children who were evacuated from London to escape the bombing came to stay in his house in the country, and he would sometimes entertain them by telling stories. When he started to write the first Narnia book, he began with the faun and the children from London. For some reason, he also kept dreaming of lions. Finally, he put the lion in the book too—and everything else followed after.

The Narnia books were wildly popular with readers. They have sold millions of copies in more than 40 languages. The stories are about ordinary kids having extraordinary adventures in a country where animals talk and trees come to life, where honor and courage are valued and justice is possible. Through them all runs a sense of magic and mystery, dominated by the mystical image of Aslan himself, the fierce and joyful lion.

Aslan's Country

C. S. Lewis never had children of his own. He married late in life, and his wife, Joy Gresham, had two little boys from a previous marriage. Sadly, she developed cancer and died only four years into their marriage. He looked after the two boys (*The Horse and His Boy* is dedicated to them) until he grew ill himself. He died in 1963 at the age of 64.

Even though C. S. Lewis was well known as a writer for adults, The Chronicles of Narnia have remained his most popular

Although Jack Lewis wrote several books for adults, it was his books for children that made him really famous.

books. Lewis wrote them because he had a story to tell, and the books work on that basic level. But they also have a Christian message about faith and values. Lewis didn't want children to be frightened or bored by Christianity, the way he was when he was a child. He wanted to capture their imaginations with powerful myths and images unlike those they encountered in church and Sunday school. Children can read the books seeing Aslan as Jesus and Aslan's country as heaven, or they can just enjoy them for the sheer fun, adventure, and joy they convey.

BOOKS

The seven books in The Chronicles of Narnia are the only books Lewis wrote for children. He suggested reading them in the following order.

The Magician's Nephew
The Lion, the Witch and the Wardrobe
The Horse and His Boy
Prince Caspian
The Voyage of the Dawn Treader
The Silver Chair
The Last Battle

C. S. Lewis: Christian and Storyteller, by Beatrice Gormley, is a good biography of Lewis, with lots of interesting pictures.

Elwyn Brooks White
(1899–1985)

The Glory of Everything

En squirmed in his seat. His wool pants were itchy. He ran his finger inside the top of his collar, trying to loosen it a bit. Then he sat on both of his hands to keep them still. The principal was reading from the Bible, something about a king, and a war, and a wind. After he finished he would call out a name, and that kid would have to walk up the stairs onto the platform and recite a poem from memory.

They were up to the M's. The kid would be a Marshall or a Matthews or a Miller. Not a White. En was nine and he'd only been called on to recite once since he started school. They seldom reached the W's before the end of term.

"But what if they make a mistake?" The chattering in his head never stopped. "M looks just like W upside down. They could get it wrong, and call on me, and—"

Sweat began to tingle on his forehead and the back of his neck. He closed his eyes, praying.

The principal closed the big Bible with a thud.

"And now I'd like to ask," he consulted a piece of paper, "I'd like to ask ..."

A roaring filled En's ears and he struggled to hear.

"El ..."

En gasped for breath.

"Eleanor ... Moore to come to the front and recite for us."

A girl shuffled up the aisle past En and mounted the steps.

"Phew," thought En, feeling suddenly cool as the sweat ran down under his collar. "That was a close one."

After school that day, he pushed hard on the big school door and walked out into the fresh, early spring afternoon. Mac sat at the schoolyard gate in his usual place. As soon as he saw En, he jumped up and nearly wagged his tail off. En gave him a friendly pat and off they went. With every step, En felt just a bit lighter.

When he got to the big house on the corner of Summit Avenue, he and Mac went around the back and into the stable. En stopped just inside the door and took a deep breath, drawing in all the wonderful smells: horses, hay, grease, and sweat. James wasn't there, so he had it all to himself.

Mac nosed around the stalls, checking out all of his own favorite smells, tail waving. En could hear pigeons cooing in the rafters and the gentle snuffling of a horse. He ambled along to the back stall, where he kept his animals.

At the moment, he had some lizards, two rabbits, a

chameleon, a turtle, and a mouse, all with their own cages. First, he filled up their water pans and made sure they all had something to eat, talking to them as he worked. Then, he drew a little stool up to the bench near the mouse's cage so he could watch it. The sounds of the stable rose and fell around him, and Mac lay

Almost everything made En nervous when he was a little boy.

across the door to the stall, with one eye closed and the other on En.

He had caught this mouse a month ago, when he was sick in bed with a cold. He had constructed a gymnasium for it, equipped with a wheel and a jungle gym. The mouse had sort of learned some tricks; it could make the wheel go and sometimes ran up and down the jungle gym. When he got over his cold, En moved the mouse out to the stable and kept up with the daily training, but the mouse seemed to lose interest.

"Maybe he needs a mate," thought En. "I could find him a wife. Then I could train both of them."

He mused about this for a while, feeding the mouse some breadcrumbs. The peacefulness of the stable crept over him, and he felt a little sleepy. The terrors of school—the assembly, the cavernous

The Glory of Everything   67

boys' washroom in the basement, the teachers with their endless questions—all faded. He didn't have to go back until nine o'clock the next morning.

En reached behind a loose board on the wall and pulled out an exercise book. Searching in his pocket for a pencil, he found half a cookie. He crumbled some off for the mouse and then ate the rest of it. He opened the book, and began to write.

I had a narrow escape at assembly today. It makes me shudder just to think about it. Mac walked me home as usual. Mouse is still reluctant to exercise and I think a mate might raise his spirits. He might want to show off for her by hanging from a bar by his tail. I'll have to see if I can catch a lady mouse tonight in the pantry. Weather continues sunny but cool. I wonder if I'll ever have a mate and want to show off for her. I could write her a poem. A poem about a mouse maybe.

A Born Worrier

Some people are born worried. Elwyn Brooks White was one of them. Even though he grew up in a well-off, happy family, he was tormented by fear. From a very young age, he had a long list of anxieties that ranged from daily terrors to bigger issues such as going to college, what he would do for a living, and the meaning of life.

He was frightened of school in general and the thought of reciting a poem in public sent him into a cold sweat. So did almost anything outside the safety of the big, comfortable house where he lived with his father and mother, two brothers, and three sisters.

Like Maud Montgomery and Jack Lewis, En White had a finely tuned sensitivity to nature. He felt intense joy outdoors—skating, canoeing, or watching animals. But he was almost too sensitive, and his keen imagination led him into some really scary

The White family lived in this big house. The stable is on the right.

daydreams. He felt small and unprotected in a huge, terrifying world. He felt a bit like—a mouse.

The Family Fortress

Like his fictional creation Stuart Little, Elwyn Brooks White was born into a perfectly normal, happy family who loved him and accepted him for who he was. They lived in Mount Vernon, a prosperous suburb of New York City. He was the sixth and last child to be raised by Samuel and Jesse White. His mother called him Elwyn, a Welsh name, but he hated it and his family called him En for short.

The Whites' large, gray house had a tower, two screened-in porches, a big garden, and a stable round the back. For En, the house was his castle, where all the terrors of the world were kept at bay. When he ventured beyond the family fortress, however, anything could happen.

When his parents announced that he was starting kindergarten, En put up a good fight, screaming, kicking, and crying. Predictably, his parents won.

Everything about school scared En. Motivated by the fear of doing badly and getting behind, he worked hard. His worst dread was of standing in front of the whole school to recite a poem at assembly. The teachers started on the first day with students whose last names began with A, and followed the alphabet through the school year. Usually they didn't make it to the W's, but it hardly mattered: En spent every assembly terrified that his name would be called by mistake. When his name did come up, it all played out just as he imagined: his knees shook, his heart beat frantically, his voice cracked, he mixed up the words, and perhaps worst of all—the audience laughed at him.

When En was a baby, the whole family gathered to have this photograph taken.

It proved what En felt deeply about the world: he was safe only at home.

A Ready-Made Band

Samuel White, En's father, was the president of a piano factory in New York City. He started as an errand boy when he was 13 and worked his way up in the company. A hard worker, conscientious and thoughtful, he brought his sense of order and good management home to his family. He took great pleasure in his clothes and he loved to talk. Samuel was proud of his position in the world and proud of his family.

 Echoes

When E. B. White created the character of the cob in The Trumpet of the Swan, *he was poking gentle fun at his father. Like Samuel White, the cob loves his wife and children dearly, and likes to talk on and on about the wonderfulness of himself and his world. Stuart Little also shares some of Samuel's characteristics: he too is a snappy dresser and has an enthusiastic, take-charge personality with an optimistic outlook on life.*

Samuel brought musical instruments home for the kids to play, and as En wrote later, with six kids they had a ready-made band. None of them was very good, but what they lacked in talent they made up for in gusto. Each child took up a couple of instruments, had some lessons, and then they made a splendid racket. Violins, guitars, drums, a cello, banjos—they composed their own music, improvised strange rhythms, and had a lot of fun.

En's mother, Jesse, was a kind, gentle woman who liked staying home with her family and didn't care for parties or visitors. White joked later that he didn't know what a dinner party was till he was 18. Jesse White took great pride in the fact that her father had been a famous painter, and she encouraged her children to express themselves.

Because En was the youngest child, as he grew up the house gradually emptied of his older brothers and sisters, who moved on to college or married life. When he was born, the closest to him in age were his sister Lillian, who was five, and his brother Stanley, who was eight. By the time he turned twelve, he was alone in the big house with his parents. He watched as his sisters and brothers took on the responsibilities of growing up, and he worried about what he would do when his time came.

Animal Friends

"   The barn was very large. It was very old. It smelled of hay and it smelled of manure. It smelled of the perspiration of tired horses and the wonderful sweet breath of patient cows. It often had a sort of peaceful smell—as though nothing bad could happen ever again in the world. "

En spent as much time as he could in the stable behind the house. That's where he kept his large collection of animals. His best friend was Mac, a collie. Mac ambled over to the school every afternoon to walk En home, and he had a special pen in the stable, lined with sheepskin to keep him warm in the winter.

En had a habit of acquiring pets. His parents weren't very enthusiastic about it, but En was determined. He liked looking after things. Polliwogs, turtles, birds, caterpillars, snakes, and pigeons ended up in his care. He was happiest when he was sitting quietly, observing his animals.

Echoes

In Charlotte's Web, *Fern sits for hours in the Zuckermans' barn, watching Wilbur. She sits very still, listening to the animals. Unlike all the other humans in the story, Fern can understand what they're saying to each other.*

Mount Vernon was not yet built up like New York City, and a pond, a stream, and a woods were within easy walking distance from En's house. His parents' only rule was: Be home for supper. En rode his bike all over the neighborhood, climbed trees, and bummed around Snake Pond, looking for frogs. In the winter he skated and played hockey on the pond. None of this scared him. Being outside in nature made him feel good.

En felt more comfortable with animals than people.

But the stable was his favorite place, and James, the coachman, became his fast friend. When En was about five, his father bought 50 chicken eggs and an incubator. When the time was right, James called the children into the stable to see them hatch. En had to stand on his tiptoes to see the new chicks poking their way out. He was enchanted by the sight of those strong little beaks cracking through the eggs and the little creatures emerging from the eggs. Three eggs didn't hatch, and James threw them away on the manure pile.

Observant little En heard some chirping, and when he investigated, he found that in the warmth of the steamy manure, the chicks had hatched after all. He ran and told James, who rescued them.

Echoes

The miracle of hatching eggs features in both Charlotte's Web *and* The Trumpet of the Swan. *Wilbur watches the goslings hatch in the barn and later rescues Charlotte's eggs and sees her 514 babies emerge. Early in* The Trumpet of the Swan, *five swan eggs hatch, observed from a distance by a quiet little boy, Sam.*

A Love Affair with Words

En felt the fascination of words almost as early as he felt the attraction to nature. His brother Stanley, eight years older, taught him to read by showing him how to sound out the words in newspapers. Stanley had a typewriter in his room, and En loved to bang out words on the clakkety keys. His other brother, Albert, kept the family's copy of Webster's dictionary on a special iron bookstand

En (the little one wearing black stockings) and his family relax on the porch at their cabin in Maine.

in his room. En made many trips to turn the pages of the huge book, looking up words he didn't understand. His father shared En's passion for words, as well as his love of nature, and after supper the two of them would put their heads together and have long, rambling conversations.

 Echoes

Charlotte's Web is a story about the power of words and the importance of choosing the right one. Charlotte likes to use big words such as "salutations," "versatile," and "magnum opus," kindly explaining their meanings to Wilbur. The words she weaves into her web save Wilbur's life.

The Glory of Everything   75

Lucy Maud Montgomery, E. B. White, and Madeleine L'Engle all began writing daily journals when they were eight or nine.

En had a clear memory of looking at a blank piece of paper he was about to write on and feeling a deep sense of belonging. He knew he would be a writer when he grew up. Writing made him feel better. It calmed his fears and made him quiet inside, the way he felt when he sat in the stable watching his animals. He began writing a journal when he was eight, taking pleasure in putting words together to describe his day, his thoughts, and his feelings. En kept a journal for 20 years.

Echoes

In The Trumpet of the Swan, *Sam writes in his diary about the swans, the eggs, foxes, and his worries about what he will be when he grows up. Some of his diary entries are taken word for word from E. B. White's childhood journal.*

August in Paradise

E. B. White, C. S. Lewis, and Lucy Maud Montgomery all used their deep connection to the natural world to enrich their books.

En suffered dreadfully from allergies—dust, horses, and pollen. His father decided that a month in the country might make En more comfortable during hay fever season, so when En was six, they started a family tradition of spending August in a cabin in Maine.

Life on the Belgrade Lakes was a far cry from the house on Summit Avenue. The simple cabin had an outdoor toilet and they ate all their meals in a nearby farmhouse. When En was 11, his father bought him a green 5-meter (16-foot) Old Town canoe, and had his name painted in white on the side. En liked to get up early in the morning while the rest of the family was asleep and go out in his canoe. The mist would be rising off the lake and everything was very quiet and calm. He found turtles, frogs, and nesting birds to observe. He felt perfectly at home, with the white birch trees outlined against the sky and the reeds at the edge of the lake stirring in the breeze.

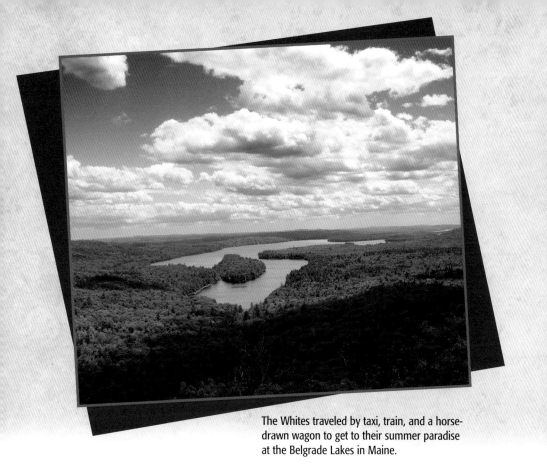

The Whites traveled by taxi, train, and a horse-drawn wagon to get to their summer paradise at the Belgrade Lakes in Maine.

 *Echoes*

Stuart Little's adventures in the sailing race on the pond in Central Park harken back to En's love of boats. In The Trumpet of the Swan, *Sam spends hour after hour on the shore of the peaceful northern lake, watching the swans.*

The only bad thing about the month in Maine was when it came to an end. Then En knew he would have to go back to school, and he worried about that.

Writing for Magazines

En liked reading books about animals or small boats, but on the whole he preferred to be outside on his bicycle, or in the stable tending to his pets. He found writing more satisfying than reading.

He was nine when he had his first publishing success, a poem printed in a women's magazine. It told the sad account of a mouse who met an untimely end in a trap, and it won a prize.

Echoes

36 years after winning a prize for a poem about a mouse caught in a trap, E. B. White wrote his famous story about a very different kind of mouse, a mouse far too clever to ever be caught in a trap—Stuart Little.

En's second publishing triumph came when he was 11. *St. Nicholas Magazine*, written for children, held writing contests for kids. The prizes were gold or silver badges. En decided he had to win one of these badges. After a friend told him that the winning stories were usually about being kind to animals, En carefully composed a tale about a walk in a snowy forest with a dog. The owner restrains the dog from chasing all the tempting squirrels, birds, and rabbits they come across.

Sure enough, his story won a prize: a silver badge. The tale was published in the June 1911 issue of the magazine. En was thrilled to see his name in print. He kept on submitting stories over the next few years, and although he received "honorable mentions" for many of them, it wasn't until he was 14 that he won another badge—this time the gold—for a piece called "A True Dog Story."

En had discovered early that he could successfully combine his love of animals with his love of writing. In high school his writing became more sophisticated and he held the position of assistant editor of the school newspaper, writing pieces about politics and social issues.

Dating Disaster

His writing may have grown more sophisticated in high school, but En remained shy and awkward around girls. His sister Lillian tried to coach him in dancing and dating, but in this one area he was a bit of a slow learner.

When he was 16, there was a girl he liked, Eileen Thomas, and he worked up the courage to ask her out on a date. He spent weeks planning exactly what he would say on the phone and what they would do. En decided that they would take the train into New York and go dancing at the Plaza Hotel and then have dinner. It was pretty ambitious for a first date. He had all the details worked out, the phone call went well, and finally the big day came. The two teenagers boarded the train for New York, arrived at the Plaza and danced. Then they had some cinnamon toast. The strain started getting to En and he suddenly decided he couldn't take any more of the stilted conversation and his intense feelings of awkwardness. He canceled the dinner and took Eileen home.

En found the sophisticated Plaza Hotel an intimidating setting for his very first date with a girl.

Echoes

*When Stuart Little stops by the sleepy town of Ames'
Crossing, he discovers a girl there who is just his size. He
asks Harriet Ames on a date. Like En, he plans it carefully
down to the smallest detail, but just like En, he gets a bit too
ambitious. He proposes to take her on a canoe ride, but
then he has to buy a canoe. The only one he can find is a
little souvenir birchbark canoe, which needs a lot of work to
make it waterproof. When Harriet arrives, everything goes
wrong. Some boys have been playing with the canoe and
messed it up. Stuart can't handle the tension as he sees all
his plans crumbling, and the date comes to an abrupt end.*

Grown-up Life

The anxieties he had as a child followed
E. B. White into adulthood. He still worried
about everything, but he continued to
find peace in nature and in writing.

En left home to go to Cornell University in Ithaca, New
York, when he was 18. He wrote for the college newspaper and
joined a writers' club. The first president of Cornell had been a
man named Andrew White. A college tradition gave the nick-
name "Andy" to anyone whose last name was White. En was
known as Andy White for the rest of his life.

After White graduated, he and a friend took off on an
extended car trip across the United States. Whenever they ran
out of money, they stopped and did odd jobs until they had
enough money to set off again. They washed dishes in restaurants, sold bug killer door-to-door, played the piano in a bar,
sold poems and stories, and finally sold one of their typewriters.
After about a year out west, White returned to New York and tried
to make a career as a writer. He worked as a reporter but he kept
quitting because he hated deadlines and he hated asking people

Grand Central Station, about 1919. White's job was to write magazine articles about big, bustling New York City.

nosy questions. When he was 26, he started writing articles for a brand-new magazine, *The New Yorker.* He ended up working for the popular magazine for the next 50 years.

White is known as one of the cleverest, wittiest, and most elegant writers of the twentieth century. His articles for *The New Yorker* were often funny, and people loved to read them. He also co-wrote a book about writing called *The Elements of Style.* It sets out some simple rules for writing well and it has become a bible for writers, students, and editors.

When he was 30, White married Katharine Angell, the fiction editor at *The New Yorker.* He had fallen in love with her while they were working together, and he wrote her love poems. She had two children from a previous marriage, and they had one child together, Joel. They split their time between an apartment in New York and a farm in Brooklin, Maine.

White kept struggling with his anxieties. He became quite fearful about his health, and often imagined he had something horrible wrong with him. Sometimes, he was so upset he had to take time off work.

When he was 46, he took off in a new direction with his career: writing children's books.

The Mouse

For about 10 years before *Stuart Little* was published, White had been amusing his nieces and nephews with stories about a mouse who acted like a human being and had all sorts of adventures. When he took some time away from *The New Yorker* in his forties, he started working these tales up into a book. Stuart Little, that valiant, adventurous, and well-dressed mouse, made his public debut in 1945. The book was an immediate success, although some grown-ups couldn't get past the strange idea of a mouse born into a human family. But young readers had no such qualms; kids loved the book and it quickly became a bestseller.

White in his office at *The New Yorker* magazine with Minnie, his dachshund.

The Pig and the Spider

As a grown-up, White kept farm animals in his barn. He always felt sorry for the pig who was butchered for bacon in the fall. He decided to write a story about a pig that got saved. Then, White became fascinated with a big, gray spider he found in the outhouse. He rigged up a light so he could watch it weave its web and lay its eggs. Slowly, the story started coming together, and soon he was writing about one of his favorite places: a barn. Wilbur and Charlotte, the geese, the sheep, and Templeton the rat came to life for him.

In 1952, White published *Charlotte's Web*. To this day, the story remains one of the most popular American children's books of all time.

The Swan

White's last children's book, *The Trumpet of the Swan*, wasn't published until 18 years after *Charlotte's Web*, when White was 70. In the meantime he was busy with his other writing, his farm, and his family. *Trumpet* took him a long time to write. White found out everything he could about trumpeter swans, just as he had researched spiders for *Charlotte's Web*.

The story about nests, eggs, birds, and true love has White's typical mix of humor, animals, magic, and excellent writing.

Barn Happiness

At the end of *Stuart Little*, the gallant little mouse decides to head north to search for Margalo. For him that direction holds the promise of wilderness and peace. For White, the North had a special allure. He always found peace in nature when he traveled north, starting with his trips to Maine when he was a boy. Later, he spent some summers working at a camp in Ontario, and then, when he found his farm in Maine, he always had his own refuge in the North.

When White was 58, he and Katharine made a permanent move to their farm in Maine. White settled into the country life

C. S. Lewis, Philip Pullman, and E. B. White all use the North in their books as a mysteriously romantic destination.

The Newbery

Charlotte's Web was named a Newbery Honor Book for 1953.

The Newbery Medal was the very first children's book award in the world. In the mid-eighteenth century, Englishman John Newbery (1713–1767) made a specialty of publishing good-quality books for children. The American Library Association created the Newbery Medal in his honor in 1922, to encourage excellence in children's writing.

The Newbery Medal is given to the best American children's book of the year, and the Newbery Honor Book title goes to the runners-up.

Two of the authors included in this book won the Newbery Medal: Christopher Paul Curtis in 2000 for *Bud, Not Buddy* and Madeleine L'Engle in 1963 for *A Wrinkle in Time.*

Christopher Paul Curtis has also won two Newbery Honor Book awards—for *Elijah of Buxton* in 2008 and for *The Watsons Go to Birmingham—1963* in 1996. Madeleine L'Engle won the Honor Book for *A Ring of Endless Light* in 1981.

he loved so well, with sheep, pigs, chickens, geese, and cows in his very own barn. He liked the slow rhythm of nature on a farm better than the rush-rush-rush of the city. White loved sailing more than almost anything, and his farm in Maine was right by the water, so he could go out in his boat whenever he wanted to.

White was awarded many honors for his writing, but he avoided going to the award ceremonies whenever possible. He never lost his early dread of standing up in front of an audience.

When White was 78, his beloved Katharine died. He spent the next seven years on his farm, writing, looking after his animals, and going sailing whenever he could. He died in 1985. Despite all his worrying, he had a long and productive life.

Like Wilbur at the end of *Charlotte's Web*, White could always find contentment in a barn, in the company of animals.

" *Life in the barn was very good—night and day, winter and summer, spring and fall, dull days and bright days. It was the best place to be, thought Wilbur, this warm delicious cellar, with the garrulous geese, the changing seasons, the heat of the sun, the passage of swallows, the nearness of rats, the sameness of sheep, the love of spiders, the smell of manure, and the glory of everything.* "

BOOKS

E. B. White wrote three books for children.

Stuart Little
Charlotte's Web
The Trumpet of the Swan

If you want to learn more about E. B. White's life, these two biographies are very good.

E. B. White: Some Writer!, by Beverly Gherman
E. B. White: The Elements of a Writer, by Janice Tingum

If you love reading books, you know
what it is like to lose yourself in a story.
Your bedroom drops away and you're
in the world of the book, side-by-side
with the hero or heroine. Your ticket
to those other worlds depends on the
power of your imagination and the
power of the words you're reading.
The best writers scoop you up and
take you on a ride that only ends on
the last page of the book.

create this
kind of mag
a writer nee
a very spec
kind of
imagination.

Madeleine L'Engle
(1918–2007)

The Outcast

Miss Hathaway held up Madeleine's history test.

"Once more, Madeleine Camp has provided us with an excellent example of how to fail a history test," she began, her mouth twisted in a half smirk. "Covered with ink blotches, half the questions unanswered, and the ones she did answer are all wrong. Take a look, children, and remember—never do what Madeleine does or you'll get an F too."

The girls sitting on both sides of Madeleine tittered. As Miss Hathaway handed the shameful sheet of paper back to Madeleine, someone whispered loudly, "The cripple strikes again," and laughter rippled through the classroom.

Madeleine kept her face blank as she took the test and shoved it into her schoolbag. The bell rang and the teacher returned to the front of the class, giving instructions about the homework as the girls gathered their belongings. Madeleine ignored her, as usual.

What was the point of doing homework? It just gave Miss Hathaway more opportunities to point out how stupid she was.

The girls brushed by her as they left the room. She slung her leather schoolbag over her shoulder and headed out, her head down to avoid meeting anyone's eyes. She knew what she would see there. It was always the same. In two years, she hadn't made one friend at this awful place. It was supposed to be one of the best girls' schools in New York, and that's why her mother had sent her here, against her father's wishes.

Madeleine never told them about Miss Hathaway's scorn, or the taunts and jeers she put up with in gym class, where she was awkward and slow, and where everyone complained loudly if she ended up on their team. Madeleine didn't tell her parents anything. She ate her supper alone in her room on a tray while her parents dined late or went out to parties or the theater. Every Sunday, the family ate lunch together, but that wasn't a time to talk about school problems. They discussed art, literature, or the latest opera production. Madeleine didn't want to spoil those meals with complaints about school.

When she got home that afternoon, the apartment was quiet. Her mother's door was closed. She was probably taking one of her long naps. Her health wasn't good, and Madeleine learned to be quiet when she came in so as not to disturb her. A rasping cough sounded from her father's study. He would be writing a theater review or a magazine article, and Madeleine knew better than to bother him when he was writing.

She walked into her little back bedroom and laid her schoolbag by the door. There it would sit, unopened, until she picked it up again on the way to school tomorrow morning. She sat down at her desk and picked up the pen that was lying there.

"I am the cripple," she said to herself. "I am the unpopular cripple." She took a deep breath and opened a notebook. At the top of the page was the title of the story she was writing: "The Strange Adventures of Annabelle Rose." Last night she had left Annabelle in a dreadful fix, tied up to a tree in the middle of a forest, surrounded by desperate bandits. Today she had to find a way for Annabelle to get loose, defeat the bandits, and release the king from their terrible clutches. She had no doubt that Annabelle would succeed in her quest. Her fearless heroine had long, curly, dark hair and flashing black eyes. She was strong and smart and there was no bandit on earth who could keep Annabelle Rose tied up for long.

A small smile turned up the corners of Madeleine's mouth as she began to write. School, Miss Hathaway, her distant parents, and even New York City all vanished as she entered her secret world. Day after day she sat at her desk, writing stories and drawing pictures. Her heroines moved gracefully through their adventures, their two legs the same length so they didn't limp. They conquered all obstacles and gathered loving friends and admirers around them. This was the real world. School and Miss Hathaway and the silent apartment were just shadows of an unpleasant dream.

Porridge without Sugar

Madeleine L'Engle's parents were married nearly 20 years before Madeleine was born. They had grown accustomed to life without a child, and when their much-longed-for baby finally arrived, they didn't see why they should change their grown-up habits. So they continued to dine late and enjoy the many attractions of New York City—opera, theater, and sophisticated parties—while Madeleine stayed at home with her nanny.

Charles and Madeleine Camp disagreed about how to bring up the baby right from the beginning. Mr. Camp wanted her to have an English childhood, where children were "seen and not heard." Mrs. Camp wanted a more American upbringing for her daughter, but Mr. Camp won the first round. Madeleine was confined to the nursery with British nanny Mrs. O'Connell. Every day, Madeleine and her nanny went out for a healthy walk in the park and ate their meals off trays in the nursery. Although Mrs. O'Connell was not given to hugs or cuddles, she did love Madeleine and managed to break some of her parents' strict rules.

Mrs. Camp didn't want Madeleine to eat sugar and would taste her porridge every morning to make sure her daughter wasn't sneaking the sweet stuff behind her back. Mrs. O'Connell foiled this by putting a spoonful of sugar in the bottom of the bowl, then filling it with porridge. Once Mrs. Camp had given her approval, the nanny stirred it up and Madeleine enjoyed her breakfast.

Madeleine's first three years at school went smoothly. She quickly learned to read and started piano lessons, which she loved. But when it came time to choose a new school for fourth grade, her parents disagreed again. Mrs. Camp wanted her to go to an exclusive private girls' school, and this time she won. This decision was to have a profound effect on Madeleine for the rest of her life.

The Outcast

Madeleine was a shy, quiet child. When she was three, she had an illness that left her with one leg shorter than the other. This gave her a slight limp, especially when she was tired. As a result, she moved awkwardly at times and did poorly at sports. Her new school placed a lot of importance on athletics, and her schoolmates groaned and made rude remarks if they were forced to have her on their team. She became known among students and staff as a stupid, clumsy child. Her teacher held up her work as examples of how not to do things. Sunk in her misery, Madeleine stopped trying and didn't do her homework.

Most people living in New York City live in apartment buildings rather than houses, often built around a courtyard, like this one.

Like many people in New York City, the Camps lived in a tall apartment building. Madeleine's bedroom was at the back, overlooking a court surrounded on four sides by other apartment buildings. She could see a flat rooftop opposite and a glimpse of sky beyond. A patchwork of lighted windows showed her people going about their daily activities, unaware that they were being observed by a small and thoughtful child.

After school, instead of doing her homework, she sat in her room by her window. She daydreamed about the people she could see across the courtyard, read books, painted pictures, and wrote stories and poems. Slowly, using her rich imagination, she created a world that provided her with all she was missing. When she was eight she began recording her thoughts and feelings in a daily journal, and this became a lifelong habit.

> *My real life was not in school but in my stories and dreams … The people I lived with in books were far more real to me than my classmates. The Madeleine I wrote about in my stories was far more my real self than the self I took to school.*

Sneaking behind the Sofa

Writing came naturally to Madeleine, who composed her first story at the age of five. Her father was a writer and a journalist. During the First World War, Mr. Camp reported news from the battlefront in Europe. His lungs were badly damaged in a mustard-gas attack, and when he returned home he had a racking cough and an illness that was never going to get better. Madeleine could not remember a time his cough didn't echo through the apartment.

Madeleine's mother also suffered from various illnesses. But when the Camps were feeling up to it they had an active social life. New York in the 1920s was buzzing with excitement. If they weren't dressing up to go to the theater or a party, they were welcoming their talented friends into their home.

Madeleine was supposed to be asleep in her room, but who could close their eyes while an opera singer warbled in the living room, or the haunting strains of a violin echoed through the hall? She would creep into the living room, and crawl behind the sofa and lie hidden, transported by the heavenly music.

In the Camp household, the arts were part of the everyday

world. From a young age, Madeleine was exposed to books, painting, theater, music, and dance. Her parents talked about art to her and to each other. She grew up believing that making art was as natural as making supper.

The Winning Poem

Meanwhile, at her dreadful school, Madeleine just gritted her teeth and got through it. She didn't put any effort into her schoolwork and kept all her good writing to herself. But in sixth grade, she decided to enter one of her poems in the school literary contest.

Her poem won—and that's when the trouble started. Madeleine's teacher declared that Madeleine must have copied the poem from somewhere else, because she was too stupid to write it herself. This time, Madeleine finally told her parents what was going on. Her mother gathered up a selection of Madeleine's writing and took it to the principal to prove that her daughter could write. The school backed down and Madeleine remained the winner of the contest.

Up until then, her parents were aware that she was unhappy, but her father had stubbornly insisted that Madeleine stay at 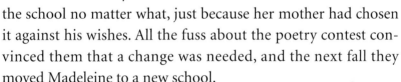 the school no matter what, just because her mother had chosen it against his wishes. All the fuss about the poetry contest convinced them that a change was needed, and the next fall they moved Madeleine to a new school.

Echoes

The wounds inflicted in that New York private school never completely healed. Somewhere deep inside, Madeleine always believed that she was stupid and awkward: a misfit. She used her vivid memories of her unhappiness in her writing. In A Wrinkle in Time, *Meg is misunderstood by the kids and the teachers at school, and she has no friends. She hates herself and the world.*

Madeleine loved dogs all her life. This picture was taken when she was 14, holding her dog Sputstzi.

At the new school, Madeleine finally had a teacher who recognized her talent. Miss Clapp encouraged Madeleine's writing and challenged her to read more difficult books. Now her stories were read to the class as examples of good writing. At last Madeleine felt appreciated and understood. She made some friends and wrote more than ever.

But her happiness was short-lived. Madeleine's father developed a severe case of pneumonia and had to go into hospital. Everyone thought he would die. Somehow he pulled through, but the doctors said he had to get out of New York. His weak lungs couldn't survive any longer in the dirty city air. Madeleine had to leave her beloved Miss Clapp and her new school and move to Europe with her parents.

A Number Instead of a Name

When summer ended, Madeleine had to go to school, and once more her parents disagreed about her education. Her mother wanted her to stay with them in France and go to a local school, but her father insisted on sending her to a Swiss boarding school. At 12 years old, Madeleine found herself saying goodbye to her parents and facing life without them.

Chatelard was an Anglican school run on strict principles. Girls were never to be left alone. They were known by their student number, not their name, and every minute of their day was scheduled. Madeleine, who was used to spending hours by herself, quickly grew desperate in the oppressive atmosphere. She tried to snatch a few minutes to write by locking herself in the bathroom, but an angry matron was soon pounding at the door, demanding to know what she was up to.

The food was dreadful and the school was never warm. The other girls had started school a week earlier than Madeleine and had already made their friends. Madeleine was once more in the position of being the weird kid whom nobody understands and nobody bothers with. Every night, she cried herself to sleep, homesick and alone. Finally, she wrote to her parents, begging them to rescue her.

When their reply finally came, it sealed her doom. After much discussion, her parents had decided that Madeleine should stay in school and make the best of it. The experience would be good for her, they said. Madeleine realized that her parents could not be relied upon to make things better for her.

Boarding-school life leaves very little room for privacy.

Echoes

In A Wrinkle in Time, *Meg's father has been missing for a year. Meg's pain and longing for her father run through everything she does. Then, after she rescues him from his captors on the planet Camazotz, he disappoints her by not making everything right. It is left to Meg to find a way through her troubles by herself. She has to face the fact that her father has faults just as she does, and is not the knight in shining armor she once believed him to be.*

Never had Madeleine felt so abandoned. It seemed impossible that she could survive in this school, where everything was regulated and anyone who was different was punished. The only place she could be alone with her thoughts was in bed at night. That soon became her only refuge. Before she went to sleep, she used her imagination to travel into the familiar landscape of her secret world. She made up stories in her head and wrote them down whenever she could.

Gradually, she learned how to enter her secret world during the day too, while she was in class. She learned how to block out everything around her and focus on her inner world. This was a skill that would prove invaluable later in her life, when she could write anywhere—on a busy train, on an airplane, in the same room as her noisy children.

Echoes

Her experiences in the strictly regulated Swiss boarding school aroused a hatred of conformity in Madeleine L'Engle that remained with her all her life. As a staunch individualist who did what she wanted to, not what people expected her to, she was acutely aware of the pressure to go along with the crowd.

On the planet Camazotz in A Wrinkle in Time, *everyone is exactly the same. All the houses and gardens are identical, and the children play ball and skip in exactly the same rhythm. The planet is controlled by an evil force that has decided that people will only be happy if they are all alike. Anyone who is different is punished. The inhabitants never feel any pain, but neither do they feel any joy. Meg is appalled by the dreariness of life on Camazotz. She realizes that in losing their individuality, the people have lost their souls.*

The town of Montreux, on Lake Geneva, where Madeleine went to boarding school. She made up stories about the glorious mountains she could see on the other side of the lake (the Alps).

Friends in Books

From the moment she learned how to read, Madeleine devoured books. She loved everything about them, even the smell. When Madeleine's mother wanted to punish her, she wouldn't let Madeleine read any books or do any writing for 24 hours. This was the worst punishment Madeleine could imagine, and she would beg her mother to spank her instead.

Madeleine didn't live near a public library, so she had a hard time getting new books. She read everything she could get her hands on, and she read her favorites over and over again. Because she lived so much in her vivid imagination, the characters in books became as real to her as the people around her. She especially loved the books written by a popular Victorian children's

Madeleine L'Engle and Christopher Paul Curtis both loved the way books smelled.

author George MacDonald: *The Princess and the Goblin, The Princess and Curdie,* and *At the Back of the North Wind.* The characters in his books were her constant companions as she lived through their adventures with them, page after page.

The character she most identified with in her reading was Emily in L. M. Montgomery's *Emily of New Moon.* Madeleine loved this book so much that for about two years she reread it every couple of months. Emily and Madeleine both wanted to be writers and spent hours alone writing out their problems and creating stories and fanciful heroines. They both had lively, dramatic imaginations and were given to long, complicated daydreams. And they both had fathers dying of lung disease.

Another author Madeleine loved was Louisa May Alcott, the author of *Little Women.* She found Alcott's life so inspiring that she read *Invincible Louisa,* her biography, again and again. Madeleine admired her courage and her dedication to her beliefs, both qualities she was to demonstrate in her own life.

The Gathering Darkness

Her father's ill health hung over Madeleine's head like a dark cloud all through her childhood. Day after day, she lived with the knowledge that sooner or later her father's ravaged lungs would give out and she would lose him. Added to this fear was her dread of another world war that would be as devastating as the one that had destroyed her father's health.

Madeleine could control what happened in her stories and daydreams, but the real world was a frightening and unpredictable place. She was haunted throughout her childhood by a sense of impending evil and uncertainty.

Feisty Louisa
Louisa May Alcott
1832–1888

Like Madeleine L'Engle and Lucy Maud Montgomery, Louisa May Alcott turned to writing to ease the pain of a difficult childhood. Louisa started a journal at age eight, using it to record her daily frustrations, her fears, her hopes, and her never-ending attempts to keep her fiery temper in check.

Louisa's parents were part of a philosophical movement called Transcendentalism, which had very high ideals about how to live in the world. Unfortunately, her father had no money and no way of making a living, so the whole family suffered extreme hunger, cold, and deprivation, with books, ideas, and their philosopher friends their only comfort.

Little Women was an idealized version of Louisa's childhood and her family. The true story of their lives would have been too depressing to make a good children's book. Even with her buoyant sense of humor, Louisa came close to despair many times in her life.

The description of Jo March in *Little Women* is very close to Louisa's personality: smart, sassy, and strong willed. Louisa determined that she would make money for her family and struggled through many poorly paying jobs before she achieved success as a writer. She worked as a governess, teacher, seamstress, laundrywoman, and servant, all in an effort to keep food on her family's table.

During the American Civil War, Louisa worked as a nurse and helped with stomach-turning operations on dying soldiers. The experience ruined her health: she caught typhoid fever in the filthy army hospitals and the doctors treated her with a form of mercury. Its poisonous effects eventually caused her death at age 55.

Although much more practical than her dreamy father, Louisa did inherit some of his idealism. She held strong convictions about injustice in the world. She fiercely opposed slavery (a runaway slave once hid in their house when she was a child) and she championed women's rights. In a world where middle-class women didn't work but married for money, she stayed single and supported her family. *Little Women* made her famous all over the world, and she wrote many popular sequels. She also wrote for adults, including thrilling adventure stories and a book about her Civil War experiences.

Louisa May Alcott's most famous books are still popular today: *Little Women*, *Little Men*, and *Jo's Boys*.

Echoes

L'Engle drew upon her childhood terrors to create the compelling and sometimes frightening worlds of her novels. The epic struggles between good and evil in her Time Trilogy could never have been written without the deep understanding she gained as a child of what it's like to be tormented by fear.

E. B. White and Madeleine L'Engle both suffered from near-paralyzing fear as children.

Charles Wallace and Meg are nearly killed by the evil Echthroi, who seek to blot out all light and goodness in the world. The Echthroi come in many forms: clouds of choking blackness, white blood cells multiplying out of control, and human beings that have given in to the dark side.

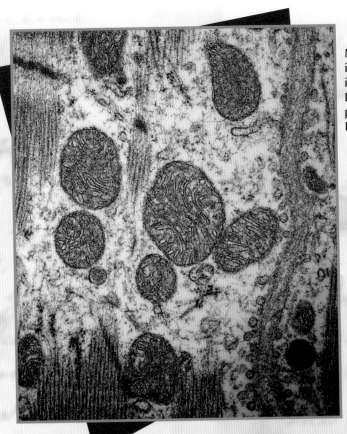

Mitochondria perform important functions inside human cells. L'Engle gave them personalities in *A Wind in the Door.*

Death

Madeleine's fears sharpened her senses. She observed life around her carefully and came to treasure moments of happiness, especially the time spent with her parents on school holidays.

After two years in Europe, her parents moved back to the United States, to live in Florida with Madeleine's grandmother. Madeleine was glad to be back where she had spent so many happy summer vacations. A long, sandy set of stairs led down to the beach from the house. She spent hours by the ocean that summer—swimming, walking, daydreaming, writing poems, and gazing at the horizon.

One night, Madeleine had a strange feeling that something bad was going to happen. She lay listening to the sounds of the house, drifting in and out of sleep. Then, suddenly, she was wide awake. She knew something was wrong. She went to her parents' room and woke them up, telling them they must go to her grandmother. When they entered the old lady's room, they found her struggling to breathe. She died within minutes from a heart attack.

All her life she had lived with the fear of death, and now it was real. Madeleine and her mother went out to swim as the sun rose over the water. The touch of the water on her skin, the blazing glory of the sunrise all around her, and her close connection to her mother all served to comfort her. If the world could continue in beauty after death, maybe she could find some meaning in it all.

Echoes

The theme of death comes up again and again in L'Engle's books. What is it? What does it feel like? How do we accept it when someone we love dies? In A Ring of Endless Light, *Vicky Austin struggles with her understanding of life and death as tragedy strikes people around her. Swimming in the ocean, she communes with dolphins who show her the joy to be found in nature and help her see that she is part of the whirling pattern of life and death in the universe.*

L'Engle wrote about the wonders of life, from the vast distances of outer space to the tiny mitochondria within cells.

E. B. White and Madeleine L'Engle were both editors of their school magazines.

The End of Childhood

In the September after her grandmother's death, Madeleine found herself once more packed off to boarding school, this time to Ashley Hall in South Carolina to begin ninth grade. Here, finally, Madeleine found her place. She threw herself into school activities, made friends, and worked hard at her schoolwork and her writing. She spent her high-school years acting in school plays and editing the school literary magazine. In her final year, she was elected president of the student council. She grew very tall (nearly two meters, or six feet) and she still tripped over her feet sometimes, but now she could laugh at herself. One year, one of her poems won the poetry prize.

In the autumn of her final year of high school, Madeleine received a disturbing letter from her mother. Her father was in hospital again with pneumonia. Not knowing what else she could do, Madeleine copied out three of her poems for him and put them in the mail. But deep inside, she had a feeling he wouldn't live long enough to read them.

The next day she was called down to the principal's office. During the night, her father's condition had deteriorated. Madeleine took the first train home, praying all the way for God to do what was best. But by the time she got home, it was too late for her even to say goodbye. Her father had died while she was praying for him on the train.

It wasn't like her grandmother's death. This time Madeleine took no comfort from the sunrise over the ocean. She didn't cry at the funeral. She froze up. On the surface, she seemed strong and calm. Madeleine pushed all her grief deep inside.

God

Madeleine returned to her busy life at school. After all the years of worrying about her father, what she most feared had now come to pass, and a numbness spread over her. She found herself grappling with the most basic questions about death: Where was her father now? What had happened to his spirit? Would she ever see him again?

Madeleine felt a deep connection to the spiritual world early in her life. As a young child, she believed in God and felt the influence of an intelligent spirit all around her. Growing up shook her beliefs. She couldn't relate to the strict, forbidding God of her Anglican boarding school. The God she experienced was the loving, mysterious force that filled the universe with joy and life, not an angry, exclusive God bent on punishing everyone who didn't believe in Him.

Madeleine eventually found God in the creative act of

writing, in her secret world where she explored the battle between good and evil, light and darkness. Her father's illness and death, her troubles at school, her loneliness, and her longing for a healthy, happy family—all these childhood experiences made lasting impressions on Madeleine and found their way into her books. So did all her basic questions about God and the meaning of life. It took her many years to discover what she believed in, and as with everything else in her life, she used her writing to find her way.

Grown-up Life

After she finished high school, Madeleine spent four years at college and then headed for New York like a homing pigeon. There she found an exciting world of actors, writers, artists, and musicians—the world she had glimpsed at her parents' parties from behind the sofa so many years ago. She wrote novels, poetry, and stories, and made her living by acting in plays.

Madeleine didn't want to cash in on her father's reputation as a writer in New York; she wanted to make it on her own. When she published her first book, she dropped her father's name, Camp, and used her first two names, Madeleine L'Engle, which were also her mother's and her great-grandmother's names.

L'Engle met Hugh Franklin, a handsome young actor, while they were touring in plays. They fell in love and got married. After a few years in New York, they left the city to live in a 200-year-old farmhouse called Crosswicks, in Connecticut. For eight years, they lived there, running a store and bringing up their children. They had a boy and a girl, and then adopted the orphaned daughter of friends who had died. Eventually, they decided to move back to New York for financial reasons, and Hugh took up his acting career again.

Is that Madeleine L'Engle or Mrs. Who? The author clowns for the camera with big crazy glasses like those worn by Mrs. Who in *A Wrinkle in Time*.

The Mysterious Universe

As she grew up and raised a family, L'Engle found that her search for God led her directly to science. She believed that the basic function of both science and religion was to explore the nature of the universe. Inspired by Albert Einstein, who had great respect for the mystery at the heart of life, she came to believe that the same creative force that nourished her writing also sparked the great scientific discoveries.

L'Engle's interest in science became a driving force in her most successful books. She used real science in her plots: Tesseracts exist, although we cannot use them for interplanetary travel the way Meg does in *A Wrinkle in Time*. The mitochondria that make Charles Wallace so sick in *A Wind in the Door* are part of our genes.

Mrs. Who, Mrs. Whatsit, and Mrs. Which, the three supernatural characters in *Wrinkle,* came to Madeleine while she was on a 10-week camping trip with her family. The rest of the story followed, inspired by Madeleine's fascination with science and God. Madeleine sent it to 24 different publishers before she found one willing to take a risk on such an unusual children's book. But the timing was perfect—in 1962, the public responded enthusiastically to the book's eccentric mix of fantasy, spirituality, and social comment. It won the highest honor for a children's book in the United States: the Newbery Medal.

L'Engle went on to write many more books. She was asked to speak and teach at conferences about science, writing, and God. Thousands of children came to know Meg, Charles Wallace, and Calvin from *Wrinkle,* as well as the characters from her other books.

L'Engle's writing broke new ground for children's books in the 1960s: she had strong, independent heroines and her themes touched on morality, God, science, and death. Perhaps to make up for her own lonely childhood, the families in her books were

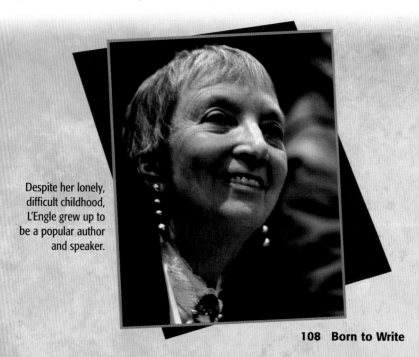

Despite her lonely, difficult childhood, L'Engle grew up to be a popular author and speaker.

large and mostly happy, with gentle, concerned fathers and strong, intelligent mothers.

Madeleine L'Engle carried her secret world with her all her life. She transformed her childhood refuge into a rich source of creativity. She wrote to try to make sense of the cruelties and injustices in life, and she wrote to express her belief in the glory and the mystery of God. L'Engle knew that many children think about the big issues of life and death. She knew from firsthand experience that the world can be a frightening and confusing place for kids, and that is what she wanted to write about. She kept writing until her death at age 89.

BOOKS

Madeleine L'Engle wrote many books for both children and adults. Her most popular are the science fiction/fantasy series about the Murry family.

A Wrinkle in Time
A Wind Through the Door
A Swiftly Tilting Planet (these three are known as the Time Trilogy) and *Many Waters*

Another popular series is about the Austin family.

Meet the Austins
The Moon by Night
The Young Unicorns
A Ring of Endless Light

If you'd like to read more about Madeleine L'Engle, her life, and her books, this is a very good biography.

Madeleine L'Engle: Author of A Wrinkle in Time, by Doreen Gonzales.

power of your imagination

W

If you love reading books, you know what it is like to lose yourself in a story. Your bedroom drops away and you're in the world of the book, side by side with the hero or heroine. Your ticket to those other worlds depends on the power of your imagination and the power of the words you're reading. The best writers scoop you up and take you on a ride that only ends on the last page of the book.

Philip Pullman

(1946–)

Spinning Stories

*T*his was the moment. When his mother had kissed them both goodnight and the bedroom door shut with a little click—this was the delicious moment—as the light slowly faded from the window and the muffled darkness drew in. Philip took a deep breath … "Now!" insisted Francis from the next bed. "Begin it now."

"Faster than a speeding bullet!" intoned Philip. "More powerful than a locomotive! Able to leap tall buildings at a single bound! Look! Up in the sky! It's a bird! It's a plane! It's—"

"It's Superman!" crowed Francis.

"When we last left Superman," said Philip in a deep, dramatic voice, just like the announcer on the radio, "he was fighting a gang of bad guys who kidnapped Lois Lane. They gagged her and tied her to a tree at the top of a waterfall and they were just chopping it down when Superman located them. Little does he know that it's a trap set by Lex Luthor to capture him once and for all. Luthor has *hidden a sliver of Kryptonite in a locket around Lois's neck and when Superman picks her up and tries to fly away with her, he will be fatally weakened.*

"Will Superman get to Lois in time to save her from a watery death? Will he discover the Kryptonite before it robs him of his super powers? To find out the answer to these and other pressing questions, listen to tonight's episode of Superman, brought to you by Pullman Pajamas. Superman! Yes, it's Superman, strange visitor from another planet—"

"Philip!" called his mother from down the hall. "Stop that nonsense and go to sleep!"

"Don't stop," begged Francis. "Whisper."

"Okay," whispered Philip softly. "So Superman grabbed the first bad guy by the throat and hurled him over the waterfall ...

"For the next 10 minutes Superman battled Luthor's henchmen. Then, in the nick of time, he caught the falling tree with Lois still tied to it and soared up up up into the blue blue sky. Suddenly the tree dipped, as if it was going to fall. Superman pushed as hard as he could, but the tree kept wobbling, and he felt his arms turning to spaghetti and a mist came up before his eyes and—"

"The Kryptonite," breathed Francis.

"The Kryptonite," continued Philip.

"The tree plunged towards the rapids. With his last ounce of strength Superman tried to turn it towards the island, but it was too late. It splashed into the water and began to spin in circles as a whirlpool dragged it towards the bottom, with Lois Lane still tied to the trunk, and Superman sinking into the deep water, down, down, his face turning green."

Here Philip stopped.

"What happened?" demanded Francis.

Philip lay back on his pillow. The window

was a pale rectangle now and shadows filled the room. He didn't see them. All he saw was Superman in the water with his green face, and Lois sputtering and choking, the tree spinning round and round. As he watched, a branch broke off and scratched Lois's face. Another branch caught at her locket and it broke with a snap and floated down past Superman to the riverbed. Superman gave a 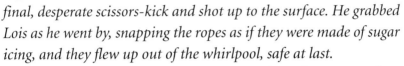 *final, desperate scissors-kick and shot up to the surface. He grabbed Lois as he went by, snapping the ropes as if they were made of sugar icing, and they flew up out of the whirlpool, safe at last.*

"Tune in tomorrow when Superman faces the unscrupulous Lex Luthor in his lair. Same time, same station," intoned Philip in his announcer voice.

He already had a couple of ideas about how the story would go on, but he wouldn't know exactly what was going to happen until about a minute before he got there. It was a bit like standing on a cliff and jumping off into the dark—and then letting the story hold him up.

"Now tell me one about Batman," said Francis.

Globetrotting

It was 1956 in a darkened bedroom in Adelaide, Australia, and Philip Pullman was 10 years old. Australia was just the latest stop in a series of homes for Philip and his little brother, Francis. They had moved from England to Rhodesia, back to England, and now here. Globetrotting was a way of life when first your father and then your stepfather flew planes for the British Royal Air Force (RAF). Except in very dangerous situations, families trailed along wherever the pilots were stationed.

Philip enjoyed traveling and he found that he liked nearly everything about Australia. The constellations were different in

In the 1950s, many parents thought comic books were a bad influence on children. Kids didn't agree.

the Southern Hemisphere, and he spotted weird and wonderful animals and trees he'd never seen before. But the best part was that he could get Batman and Superman comics. In England, American comic books were considered too violent for children, so they were banned. But in Australia, not only could Philip and Francis read all about the latest exploits of the superheroes, they could listen to radio broadcasts with live actors taking the parts of Superman, Lois Lane, and Jimmy Olsen.

Television had yet to take over the world, and radio offered a number of ongoing series the boys followed avidly. As well as *The Adventures of Superman*, they listened to *Clancy of the Outback*, about a cowboy, and another series that featured a resourceful kangaroo. The brothers couldn't get enough of these exciting stories, so Philip began a nighttime ritual of inventing more adventures for Superman and the kangaroo.

Philip Pullman later said that these first forays into story-telling gave him a taste of the thrill of invention. He loved making everything fit. Sometimes he would bring back a stray character at the close of the story and give him a role to play. And he always enjoyed finding just the right ending.

Philip may have discovered the excitement of creating a good story when he was 10, but his whole childhood laid the groundwork for the writer he would become. He lost his father, and then his mother stepped out of his life for a couple of years. He moved through different schools and different countries, living first with his parents, then with his grandparents, and finally with his stepfather and new brothers and a sister. Everything that happened to him took root in his imagination and eventually made its way into his books, one way or another.

Fighter Pilot Father

When Philip was six, he went with his mother and his brother, Francis, to live in Southern Rhodesia, a British colony, where his father was posted with the RAF. Philip didn't see a lot of his father, who spent most of his time in his club when he wasn't flying air-planes. But sometimes Alfred Pullman would swoop home and gather his son up and take him along. Philip liked the way the club smelled: a masculine, grown-up aroma made up of leather chairs, beer, and cigarettes. Alfred gave Philip sips of beer (which the boy liked) and once he handed over a whole package of ciga-rettes to his son. His father thought the cigarettes would make Philip sick and cure him of wanting to smoke, but they had the opposite effect: the boy smoked them all with great enjoyment.

A busy street scene in Rhodesia, Africa (now Zimbabwe), where Philip lived in the 1950s.

His father's world seemed to be one where danger and adventure went hand in hand. Alfred took his small sons to a boxing match in the African compound, where two men battled it out. The Pullmans picked the fighter they wanted to win and cheered him on.

It wasn't long before the Pullmans were on the move again. Audrey and the children went home to England to stay with her parents in Norfolk. Alfred remained in Africa, flying missions for the RAF over Kenya. Kenya was another African British colony, where a group of rebels that came to be called the Mau Mau were fighting against British rule. The RAF was involved in the fighting, and Alfred Pullman was in the thick of it.

 *Echoes*

In The Subtle Knife, *Will grows up without a father. His mother tells him that his father was first an officer in the Royal Marines and then he set off as a brave explorer on expeditions to unknown corners of the earth. Will daydreams about finding his father and having exciting adventures together.*

Falling out of the Sky

Philip was happy to be settled once again in the big rectory in Drayton, Norfolk, with his grandparents. His grandmother made the most delicious fried bread in England and his grandfather, an Anglican minister, told wonderful stories, many of them from the Bible.

C. S. Lewis, Madeleine L'Engle, and Philip Pullman were brought up in the Anglican Church (a branch of Christianity), and as they grew up, they all questioned these early beliefs.

Francis and Philip loved to play in the garden, and that's where they were the day the news came. Their grandmother called them into the house and told them their father was dead. His plane had crashed in Kenya. Philip would later remember seeing his mother crying, but he and his brother went back out to play. It took a while for them to realize what had happened. Their father had always been a rather remote figure, and now he was even more distant. Now he was gone.

Because he had died in the service of his country, Alfred Pullman was awarded a medal: the Distinguished Flying Cross. A few months after his death, Audrey and her two sons were invited to Buckingham Palace to a special ceremony to receive the medal. The family got all dressed up for the occasion: Francis and Philip wore gray shorts and jackets, and their mother wore an elegant black dress, as befitted a widow. A man in uniform greeted them

Echoes

In The Subtle Knife, *Will's father disappears when he is a young child. He can't remember him, but he still misses him. He longs for his father to take over and make everything right.*

at the palace and taught them how to bow to the Queen and what to say.

The Queen came in and shook their hands and everyone was extremely polite. She gave Audrey the medal in a little blue case, and then they left. Outside, photographers were waiting to take their picture for the newspapers.

Philip believed his father was a war hero. It was not until he grew up that he learned the truth: the fighting in Kenya was not as simple as the good guys against the bad guys. Both sides did ugly things, and Alfred's death was not the heroic sacrifice he had once thought it was. He also discovered that because his father had been dating other women and had many debts, his mother had been ready to get a divorce at the time Alfred was killed. But during his childhood, his father remained a dimly remembered, valiant hero.

Blue Grass Mother

After her husband's death, Audrey Pullman decided to leave the children in Norfolk and move to London to find work. She got a job at the British Broadcasting Corporation, the radio and television company run by the British government. Sometimes the boys visited her in her flat in Chelsea, a fashionable area of the city. Her life seemed very glamorous to Philip: she always wore the same exotic perfume, called Blue Grass, and she dressed in lovely dresses with hats and gloves to match. Her friends drove in sports cars and everyone seemed happy and sophisticated.

Echoes

When Lyra goes to live with Mrs. Coulter in The Golden Compass, *she is seduced by the luxury and beauty of her upscale London world. Everyone wears beautiful clothes, eats delicious food, and talks about power politics and love affairs.*

Audrey Pullman could be a difficult person to be around. Sometimes she was very cold, turning off her affection as if it were a tap. Her entire life, it seemed, had been a series of things going wrong. In 1930s England, girls were expected to grow up and marry rather than have a working career, and many people didn't think they needed as much education as boys. Audrey resented the fact that her parents had sent her brother to school but not her. When her marriage failed and Alfred was killed, she set out to make a new life for herself, but she was filled with bitterness.

Echoes

Philip Pullman borrowed some of his mother's characteristics when he created Mrs. Coulter: her coldness and her preoccupation with herself. Pullman says that Mrs. Coulter is one of his favorite characters—he loves her wickedness and strong instinct for survival.

Philip and Francis were quite content to live in the Drayton rectory with their loving grandparents. Wherever they had traveled, they had always come back here, and it felt like home. The house had a marvelous dress-up box with costumes from church pageants. School was a bit difficult at first, because they were the new boys, and shy. But after a while, they found their place.

Philip adored his grandfather, who became the center of his world. Reverend Merrifield had a strong sense of right and wrong, which he imparted to his grandsons. Philip listened spellbound to his stories. It was here in the big rectory, listening to his grandfather, that Philip

Philip sailed to Australia on an ocean liner like the *Orcades,* shown here steaming into Sydney harbor.

first began to sense the power that stories have. They picked him up and transported him to a different time and place. The best stories had something true at their heart, something important for him to know.

The family's quiet, peaceful life in Norfolk came to an end when Philip was nine. Audrey married another RAF pilot, who had been a friend of Alfred's in Rhodesia. He was kind to his stepsons and they were on their best behavior around him, but it took a while for the boys to accept him. It was another huge shift in their lives, one that would take them to the other side of the world.

Holiday at Sea

Today you can fly from London, England, to Sydney, Australia, in 24 hours. In the 1950s, it was much more common to go by ship, and it took 24 days. The ship made its stately progress through the Mediterranean Sea, along the Suez Canal and the Red Sea to the Arabian Sea and the Indian Ocean, and finally docked in Australia. The world seemed a bigger place then: a huge panorama of endless shorelines, exotic ports, and limitless horizons. Philip drank it all in.

Echoes

In the His Dark Materials trilogy, everyone is always traveling, covering vast distances. No destination is easily reached. The reader gets the sense of immense space and distance in each separate world.

In The Golden Compass, *Lyra and the gypsies sail to Lapland and then trudge across the wilderness to Bolvangar. Then Lyra travels by balloon to Svalbard, the land of the bears, in the Arctic Circle. Will and Lyra travel from world to world in* The Subtle Knife *and everywhere they want to go takes them days to reach. The same is true in* The Amber Spyglass, *where Mary Malone must travel over the plains in the world of the Mulefa, and Will and Balthamos the angel take a long journey down a river, over mountains, and through a forest.*

Life on board ship was different from life anywhere else. Time slowed down: every day was the same, but every day was different as the ship moved through climates and time zones. It was a holiday at sea, with a steady stream of wonderful meals

and entertainment. Stopping at exotic ports in the Middle East and India, Philip caught a glimpse of foreign life that made a deep impression on him.

The big event on board ship was the food: even a hungry hobbit or a ravenous nine-year-old boy would be satisfied by at least six meals a day. They started with a mini-breakfast of tea and biscuits, brought to the cabin by a steward. Breakfast was an extravaganza, with hot dishes and every kind of bread imaginable. Second breakfast came in the middle of the morning, when stewards appeared with either ice cream (when it was hot) or beef tea (when it was cold). A substantial lunch was followed a few hours later by an elegant tea of little sandwiches, pastries, and cake, served to tinkling piano music in one of the ship's lounges. Dinner was large and formal, and then there was a late snack for anyone who stayed up to dance.

Every time the ship docked, the boys caught a glimpse of a foreign country: on the quayside people were speaking a different language and the walls were covered with unfamiliar advertising for brand names they'd never heard of. When the boat stopped in Port Said, Egypt, magicians came on board and did tricks involving live chicks. As the ship moved slowly through the Suez Canal, they saw camels and palm trees on the shore, and Arabs wearing long robes. The weather became very hot.

A great deal of fun came with the crossing of the equator. It was a tradition on board ship to perform a ceremony featuring King Neptune, master of the seas, who appeared with mermaids and sea horses beside the pool, ready to dunk new travelers into the water to mark the momentous Crossing of the Line. The boys were enthusiastically dunked, and then swore an oath to King Neptune, and received a certificate.

Philip received a certificate something like this one after he was dunked in the swimming pool when his ship crossed the equator.

All his shipboard adventures fed Philip's imagination. Partway through the voyage, he and Francis came down with scarlet fever and were confined to their cabin for a few days until they got better. They had books and board games for entertainment, as well as construction kits. Soon they were building forts and castles and engaging in extended warfare. Some of the battles went on for days.

In the Batcave

One day in Australia, Philip's stepfather bought him a Superman comic and it changed his life. Philip fell head over heels into the world of Superman, Batman, Dick Tracy, and Captain America—and he never wanted to leave it.

He devoured comics. He loved the way the cheap paper turned yellow with age. His favorite was Batman, and he found himself yearning to immerse himself in the story—the pictures, the settings, the characters, the words. He wanted to be the creator of this fabulous, thrilling world: he wanted to write the stories himself.

This was when he began telling stories to Francis at night, when he could fill the dark room with the images of his superheroes. He imitated the radio shows right down to humming the musical introductions. Night after night he spun his stories, following his instinct and discovering what worked and what didn't. In that darkened bedroom in Adelaide, Philip Pullman began his career as a master storyteller.

There was lots of other reading material in his life besides comics. He liked books of all kinds, even grown-up books. But his favorite children's books ran from Arthur Ransome's *Swallows and Amazons* to *Emil and the Detectives* by Erich Kästner, *The Magic Pudding* by Norman Lindsay (which he still calls the funniest book in the world), to Tove Jansson's *Moomin* books and *A Hundred Million Francs* by Paul Berna.

Echoes

There was one illustration in A Hundred Million Francs *that stuck in Philip's head: a tough-looking French girl with blond hair and a leather jacket. The image of this wonderful, reckless girl was his first glimpse of Lyra.*

Running Wild in Wales

After two years in Australia, Philip's family was on the move again: this time to Llanbedr, a village in Wales. Here they settled down for good. The family grew: soon he had a new little brother and a sister, and his stepfather's son came to live with them. They all got

Philip spent his teenage years in Llanbedr, a little Welsh village nestled in a valley between these patchwork-covered hills.

on fairly well, and Philip spent more and more time with his friends rollicking around the Welsh countryside, raising hell.

The boys were free to go wherever they wanted—to the beach to swim, along the rivers to climb the waterfalls, to the railway line to experiment with flattening pennies under trains, to the woods to brave the horrors of the haunted "Hanging Tree." They got up to mischief whenever possible, teasing a farmer's pig, spying on lovers in bus shelters, planting fireworks on the roof of the women's public washroom. They engaged in spitting contests from the school train window and grass-bomb fights at night in the darkened fields. They even broke into an abandoned house and found a Bible and a set of false teeth on the table. Life was good.

Paradise Lost

Paradise Lost was Pullman's inspiration for the His Dark Materials trilogy. The poem, written by Englishman John Milton in 1667, tells the story of how Satan works against God to overthrow his creation and have Adam and Eve cast out of Paradise.

Pullman took the name for his trilogy from the following stanza, where Satan stands in hell and begins to plan his campaign. He is surrounded by the raw material God used to create Earth and Man.

> *Into this wild abyss,*
>
> *(The womb of nature and perhaps her grave,)*
>
> *Of neither sea, nor shore, nor air, nor fire,*
>
> *But all these in their pregnant causes mixed*
>
> *Confusedly, and which thus must ever fight,*
>
> *(Unless the almighty maker them ordain*
>
> *His dark materials to create more worlds,)*
>
> *Into this wild abyss the wary fiend*
>
> *Stood on the brink of hell and looked a while*
>
> *Pondering his voyage …*
>
> *(Paradise Lost,* Book II, Lines 910–19)

Philip loved to wander in the woods with his friends. This ancient bridge crosses a mountain stream outside Harlech, a nearby town.

Poetry and Art

And all the time, Philip was reading. His English teacher, Enid Jones, recognized his growing passion for words, and she guided him to some wonderful books. She introduced him to *Paradise Lost*, an epic poem by John Milton about the struggle between heaven and hell. Reading it, Philip felt the same thrill he had experienced with the Batman comics, only this sensation was stronger, deeper—it made his skin tingle and his heart beat faster.

PARADISE LOST made a lasting impression on both C. S. Lewis and Philip Pullman when they were boys.

Philip began a lifelong love affair with poetry. He memorized it by the bucketful. He spent hours composing poetry, using very structured forms and complicated rhyming schemes.

> *When I first became aware that … words had weight and color and taste and shape as well as meaning, I began to play with them, like a little child putting colored marbles into patterns.*

Philip went to high school in Harlech, about eight kilometers (five miles) from his home in Llanbedr.

Philip was definitely an artsy kind of teenager. Not only did he love poetry, but he played the guitar and loved to draw. He was in the academic stream at school, so he couldn't take art lessons, but he had a strong desire to draw the landscape he saw around him.

In the small village in Wales, there weren't any museums or art galleries, or even a library with a good selection of books about art. One Christmas, Philip was given money to buy a book and he purchased a large volume called *A History of Art*. The book became his art teacher. He studied all the pictures intensely, and began to draw, learning from the book. He drew all the time, concentrating on the lovely Welsh countryside.

Echoes

When he grew up, Pullman kept drawing. In some editions of the His Dark Materials books, his illustrations appear at the beginnings of chapters.

Grown-up Life

When Philip finished school, he wrote the entrance exam for Oxford University and won a scholarship to go there. No one in his family had ever been to university before, and he was enthusiastic about this big step. He loved the beauty of the old buildings, but he soon found that he didn't enjoy his courses very much. He was taking English literature, but what he really wanted to do was learn to write. After university, he wrote a novel and worked at odd jobs until he finally decided to go back to school to qualify as a teacher. Then he spent 12 years teaching 12- and 13-year-olds, in English middle school.

The students who had Mr. Pullman for English and drama were lucky indeed. His method of teaching the Greek myths was to tell them the stories. By this time, Pullman had honed his storytelling skills, and he kept his students on the edge of their seats with his dramatic tales of the exploits of the Greek gods and goddesses. He also taught drama, and threw himself into it with energy and dedication. Pullman wrote plays especially for his students, and then directed marvelous productions, with elaborate costumes, scenery, and special effects—like fireworks!

He so enjoyed writing children's plays that he started writing novels for children, and there he found his calling.

Pullman married and had two children, and eventually his writing made enough money that he could quit full-time teaching. His books were

To create thi
kind of magi
a writer need
a very specia
kind of
magination.

The Whitbread Book of the Year has always been awarded to books written for adults, until Pullman made history when *The Amber Spyglass* won it in 2001.

very successful, but it was with the His Dark Materials series that he achieved worldwide recognition. Now his books have sold more than 7 million copies and have been translated into 37 languages.

Among the many awards he has won for his writing, the Whitbread Book of the Year Award in 2001 stands out, given to *The Amber Spyglass.* This was the first time this honor was bestowed upon a children's book. That's because adults like Pullman's books too. Some grown-ups are embarrassed about reading children's books in public. To help them out, a separate edition of the His Dark Materials series was published with a more grown-up cover.

Turning Paradise Upside Down

Although *Paradise Lost* was the inspiration for the His Dark Materials trilogy, Pullman has not simply rewritten Milton's story. Instead, he has turned it upside down. Although the battle is still between good and evil, it is not always clear which side a character is fighting on. Will and Lyra (Adam and Eve) are definitely the good guys, but Lord Asriel (Satan) is harder to figure out. Sometimes he seems to be doing the right thing for the wrong reason. And the Authority (God) is just another upstart angel with a plan to rule the world. Like the Tree of Knowledge, Dust is the life force, but it is more a force for good than for evil.

By taking the centuries-old Christian beliefs, turning them upside down, and giving them a good shake, Pullman has caused a lot of controversy. He has stated very clearly that he himself does not believe in God. People have accused him of "killing God," and some say his books are dangerous.

But, like C. S. Lewis and Madeleine L'Engle, who were Christians, Pullman takes a very firm moral stand in his books. His characters, like living human beings, have both good and bad in them, and they have to make choices. As the plots work themselves out, it becomes very clear which is the right path for characters to take and which is the wrong path.

At the end of *The Amber Spyglass,* Pullman talks about something he calls "the republic of heaven." He believes that

Books by Philip Pullman, C. S. Lewis, and Madeleine L'Engle have all caused controversy because of the authors' beliefs about religion.

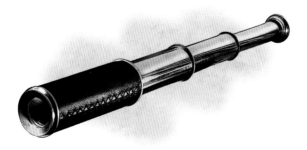

Ancient Harlech Castle, built in 1289, loomed above the town where Philip went to school.

people must make the most of their lives on earth, because there is no life after death. If people live with a sense of right and wrong, they can help to create a world where people can live peaceful and fulfilled lives. Pullman believes that joy can be experienced in this life. Rather than waiting for an elusive "kingdom" of heaven in the next life, people can create a more democratic "republic" of heaven right here on earth.

Despite the controversy surrounding Pullman's books, children and adults continue to enjoy reading them, and Pullman continues to write more. Like that little boy in the dark bedroom in Adelaide, he takes great delight in spinning his stories, weaving all the pieces together, and making everything fit, while his audience waits breathlessly for the next installment.

BOOKS

Pullman has written more than 25 books. Here is a small sampling.

His Dark Materials:
The Golden Compass
The Subtle Knife
The Amber Spyglass

I Was a Rat! or The Scarlet Slippers
The Firework-Maker's Daughter
The Ruby in the Smoke

Susan E. Reichard has written a very detailed biography of Philip Pullman, called *Philip Pullman: Master of Fantasy*. It includes an interview with the author.

Wr

power of your imagination

If you love reading books, you know what it is like to lose yourself in a story. Your bedroom drops away and you're in the world of the book, side-by-side with the hero or heroine. Your ticket to those other worlds depends on the power of your imagination and the power of the words you're reading. The best writers scoop you up and take you on a ride that only ends on the last page of the book.

to or else to kind of ima a writer ne a very spec kind of imagination

Christopher Paul Curtis
(1953–)

The Boy in the Library

*T*he book about the Civil War smelled sweet and musty—
*that old-book smell Chris loved. The pages crackled as he
turned them. Paintings showed soldiers dying in horribly
interesting ways.*

*The library was always peaceful. Around him, kids were
reading or talking in hushed voices. Nobody yelled or laughed or
jumped around. They all knew better. Anyone who made a noise
that was just a little bit too loud would have a librarian on their
case in a flash.*

*Chris looked out at the trees on the big library lawn. It was
September, and a few were just starting to turn red. His regular
Saturday visit to the library felt particularly peaceful after all the
hullabaloo yesterday. He started to smile. Yes, he got in really big
trouble, but it was worth it …*

*The fun started when his sixth-grade teacher left the class-
room, telling them to keep quiet and do their arithmetic. The door*

had barely shut on Mr. Harvey when Chris whipped a set of water-colors out of his desk and gave Marjory Williams a big, friendly grin.

"Want to have red fingernails, Marjory? Just like a real glamour girl?"

She took a little persuading, but not too much, and soon he was holding her wrist steady and painting her nails. It worked real good if he didn't add too much water, and he had to say, her nails were looking pretty fine, and all the kids were crowding around and watching and making comments and then suddenly they were quiet and he looked up and there was Mr. Harvey, with a real mad look on his face.

"I told you kids to do your arithmetic!" yelled the teacher. "I won't have this kind of behavior in my classroom. Christopher, we're going straight to your mother and we'll see what she has to say."

Chris dropped Marjory's hand like it was on fire, jumped up, and ran out the door. He ran all the way home—five blocks—not stopping until he burst into the kitchen.

"Momma!" he gasped, hanging on to the door so he didn't fall down in a heap, "Momma, don't listen to him! I was just fooling around! Don't listen to him!"

His mother turned from the stove, where she had been stirring some soup for lunch.

"What's wrong, Chris? Don't listen to who?"

But it was too late. There were pounding footsteps on the front porch and then Mr. Harvey burst in through the kitchen door. He was panting too, and sweat was pouring down his face.

"Mrs. Curtis," he choked, "Mrs.

Curtis, I won't stand for it! Your son… your son…"

His mother grabbed a glass and filled it with water.

"Just sit down now, Mr. Harvey," she said. "Sit down and catch your breath. Then you can tell me all about what my son has done this time." She shot Chris a look that made his knees weak all over again …

In the library, Chris laughed out loud, remembering how mad his mother had been. Now that it was all over, it was pretty funny. A passing librarian frowned at him and he stifled his laughter.

"Chris?" whispered his sister, sitting down beside him and looking at his book. It was open at a picture of wounded soldiers in a hospital. One was having his leg cut off with a saw.

"Ewww," she said, and plopped her library books on top of it. "Chris?"

"Yeah, what?" he said.

"Is it true what you said last night? That someday you are going to write a book?"

"Yup."

"Really?" said Cydney. "A whole book, all by yourself? What would you write about?"

Chris thought about running home with Mr. Harvey right behind him all the way. He thought about late last night, when he climbed out the window while his parents were watching TV. He thought about the thrill that ran through him from the top of his head to the tips of his toes as he crept through the shadows in the big, dark field behind the house. Then he thought about that freezing look in his mother's eyes when he knew he was in for it.

He grinned at his little sister. "I'll think of something," he said.

Chris as a baby with his older sister, Lindsey, and his mother, Leslie Curtis.

King of Mischief

When it came to mischief in the Curtis family, Chris was king. The second oldest of five children, Chris was always on the lookout for fun and there was nothing he enjoyed more than teasing the life out of the other members of his family. He dubbed his younger sister Cydney "Mother Superior" because she was always running to tell their parents about his latest wrongdoing.

Christopher Paul Curtis and Philip Pullman both got up to serious mischief as kids. Chris liked to sneak out the window at night to play, and Philip waged grass-bomb fights with his friends in the dark.

Echoes

You can't read very far in a book by Christopher Paul Curtis without starting to grin. His wicked sense of humor always comes through loud and clear. Even when the character is a homeless orphan who is unloved and abused by the people around him, like Bud, in Bud, Not Buddy, *you will find yourself laughing your head off most of the way through the book.*

His mother usually responded with the universally chilling words, "Wait till your father gets home!" Herman Curtis played the role of the disciplinarian in the family, but his wife, Leslie, could be just as scary. Mr. and Mrs. Curtis had very firm ideas about bringing up children, including going to bed at 6:30 p.m., doing regular chores, and showing respect to your elders.

All the Curtis kids hated the rules, but because the strict discipline went hand in hand with a lot of love and security, they were a boisterous, happy bunch. Unlike most of the other authors in this book, Christopher Paul Curtis did not suffer any tragic loss in his childhood. He always knew he was well loved and safe.

Echoes

All the books by Christopher Paul Curtis echo his childhood experience of the importance of a strong, loving family. In The Watsons Go to Birmingham—1963, *the family pulls together to survive some shocking events.* Bud, Not Buddy *is about Bud's quest to find a family, and in* Elijah of Buxton, *Elijah leaves the safety of his home to try to help a family separated by the cruelty of slavery.*

There was one big shadow in Chris's life. Most of the time, it remained in the background and he didn't think about it, but every so often something would happen to remind him. That shadow was racism. Although Chris was born nearly 100 years after slavery was abolished, in the 1950s most African Americans were still treated like second-class citizens.

Racism at Work

The Curtis family lived in an all-black neighborhood in Flint, Michigan. Chris rarely saw any white people. Many of his neighbors worked at the car factories that Flint is famous for. Others

were teachers, doctors, lawyers, and storekeepers. In the 1950s and 1960s Flint had a reputation as a good place to live for African Americans: they could find jobs that paid well and they could live in clean, safe neighborhoods.

Chris was born on May 10, 1953. His older sister, Lindsey, was two. Up until then, Herman Curtis had been trying to make a living as a podiatrist—a foot doctor. It wasn't a very well-known profession and business wasn't too good. White people didn't often go to a black doctor. Herman just didn't have enough patients to make a living, especially now that his family was getting bigger. Leslie Curtis had been to college but, like most women in the 1950s, once she had kids she stayed home to look after them.

So Herman went job hunting. He applied for a job in management at the Buick factory, one of the biggest employers in Flint. He quickly found out that the company wouldn't hire African Americans for anything except factory work. Despite his education and his ability, Herman had to start off on the factory floor at an hourly wage, just because of the color of his skin.

Chris plays with his dad, Herman Curtis.

Second-Class Citizens

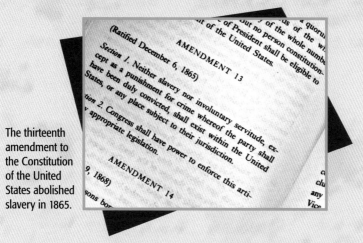

AMENDMENT 13

(Ratified December 6, 1865)

Section 1. Neither slavery nor involuntary servitude, except as a punishment for crime whereof the party shall have been duly convicted, shall exist within the United States, or any place subject to their jurisdiction.

Section 2. Congress shall have power to enforce this article by appropriate legislation.

AMENDMENT 14

The thirteenth amendment to the Constitution of the United States abolished slavery in 1865.

One hundred years after slaves were freed as a result of the American Civil War, African Americans were still being treated as second-class citizens in many parts of the United States.

Most African Americans lived in their own neighborhoods, with their own schools and local businesses. Many jobs were closed to them. They made less money, they were often poor, and they didn't have the same educational opportunities as other Americans. Because their schools didn't have as much money as white schools, they couldn't hire the best teachers, and books and school supplies were often hard to come by. In big cities, black neighborhoods developed into ghettos, where poverty and poor living conditions gave rise to violence.

In the southern states it was even worse. Segregation laws kept African Americans completely separated from white Americans. Black people were forced to eat at separate restaurants, use separate restrooms, drink out of separate water fountains, and ride at the back of the bus. All schools were either white or black. Laws prevented most African Americans from voting. Anyone who tried to change the laws or spoke out against segregation risked violence at the hands of white people who hated black people and didn't want them to have the same rights as other Americans.

Early to Bed

Now that Herman had regular work in the factory, the family was okay for money. Herman and Leslie Curtis had three more children—Cydney, David, and Sarah. The Curtises lived in a pleasant neighborhood where people looked out for each other, and everyone knew who you were and where you lived. If Chris was misbehaving two streets away, the nearest adult would give him heck and send him home. Like the time he arrived on the porch with a beautiful big bunch of tulips for his mother. Two minutes later, an irate neighbor was complaining on the phone: she'd recognized Chris as he sauntered down the street after stripping all the spring blooms from her front garden.

His parents had high expectations, and the kids had to follow the rules. One of the hardest was bed at 6:30 p.m. Every night until he was about 12, Chris had to go to bed right after supper. Kids outside would be playing ball, laughing, riding their bikes, while Chris was lying in bed listening to them. Mrs. Curtis believed that growing children needed their sleep.

C. S. Lewis, E. B. White, Madeleine L'Engle, and Christopher Paul Curtis all grew up in houses that were overflowing with books.

There was only one way to postpone "lights out": if the kids were reading in bed, they could stay up longer. Needless to say, they all read a lot. It wasn't hard in that house, because both Mr. and Mrs. Curtis loved reading and the house was full of books.

One night, Mr. Curtis gathered the kids together and told them he had a surprise for them. He took them down the hall and showed them a new bookcase, filled with red and gold volumes of the *World Book Encyclopedia*. He looked down solemnly at the children, peering over the top of his glasses. "I paid more than $300 for these books," he said, fixing his eyes on Chris. "If I find one torn page, one crayon smudge, or one pencil mark on them, I'm gonna kill someone."

Chris (about three), Lindsey, and Cydney visit Santa.

To create this kind of magic a writer needs a very special kind of imagination.

The kids were suitably impressed, and started looking at the books, very carefully. The *World Book*s were full of all kinds of information about just about everything. Chris liked looking at the anatomy pages. They had plastic overlays and you could see right inside the human body. Mr. Curtis also bought the *Childcraft Encyclopedia*, which included poetry and stories as well as useful information for school projects.

Every room in the Curtis house had books in it. One book Chris went back to again and again was his father's copy of *Gray's Anatomy*. Medical students studied this book to learn about the human body, and Chris never got tired of looking at the pictures. He knew all the names of bones and that's why he called his imaginary superhero "Ulna Boy," after the elbow bone.

Lindsey, Chris, Cydney, and David line up before going to the John Kennedy rally in 1960. Kennedy was running for president and many people hoped he would help make conditions better for African Americans.

The Curtis family also bought lots of magazines, and Chris read them all: *Time*, *Newsweek*, *Life*, and *Sports Illustrated* had interesting stories and really great pictures. *Mad* magazine kept him in stitches with its crazy jokes. He loved comics so much that when he came home from school and his mother gave him a dime to go buy candy, he spent it on DC comics instead: he couldn't get enough of Superman and Batman. He had a friend who collected Marvel comics, so when he wanted to read about Spider-man and the Incredible Hulk he went to his friend's house.

Philip Pullman and Christopher Paul Curtis both loved comics— especially Superman and Batman.

A Bigger World

Mr. and Mrs. Curtis knew that sooner or later all their kids would have to deal with racism. At first, it wasn't a big issue, because the family lived in an all-black neighborhood. But they wanted the kids to know what the bigger world was like. In the 1950s and

1960s, there were racial issues that were erupting into violence all over the United States. It was inevitable that their kids were going to come up against injustice and prejudice based on the color of their skin.

There were restaurants and banks in Flint that wouldn't hire African Americans. Herman took his kids to demonstrations to protest against this discrimination. Chris saw people getting spat on and called names because of their color. His parents believed this was an important lesson for him, and he never forgot it.

The Curtises wanted their children to learn how to be good citizens. They didn't want them growing up hating white people. They taught them how to live in a better world, a world they believed was coming.

Echoes

In Bud, Not Buddy, *when Bud visits Hooverville, the camp of unemployed workers and their families, he notes that although the people are all different colors, they all look shades of orange in the firelight. They're all united by their troubles. Only one family sits apart—a white family who can't accept help from the others because they are too proud.*

In Love with Libraries

As a man who cared a lot about workers' rights, Herman Curtis took an active part in his local autoworkers union. When he was elected union representative, he started the habit of going to the library every Saturday to research labor laws. He took the kids along.

The Flint library on Kearsley Street was brand

new; built in 1958, it was a long, two-story building, with many large windows looking out on a big front lawn filled with trees. There was a special children's section with low shelves where kids could reach the books, and little tables where they'd feel comfortable reading.

It was here that Chris began his lifelong love affair with libraries. He loved everything about the library: the way it looked, the way it smelled, the way all the books were lined up on the shelves; he knew there were hundreds of stories there just waiting to be discovered.

Echoes

In Bud, Not Buddy, *Bud uses the local library as his refuge. Just like Chris, he appreciates the library smells and enjoys looking at gory pictures of the Civil War.*

Only one thing bothered him. There were hardly any books about kids like him. Nearly all the stories were about white kids, written by white authors. Their families and their lives were different from his. Chris would have to wait a long time to read children's books by African-American authors. The world had to get a little closer to the one his parents dreamed of.

Chris read everything he could get his hands on and never felt quite as happy as on those Saturdays in the library. When his father told him he was old enough to go

The children's section of the Flint Public Library, the way it looked when Chris went there every Saturday with his father.

to the adults' section, he was filled with pride. He felt so good in the library that, when he grew up, he went to a library to write his books.

Friday Was Fight Day

It didn't take long for Chris's teachers to discover that he was a bright boy. He loved school, and he did very well. In third grade, he and a little girl were the first African Americans in the public school system in Flint to be included in a special program for gifted children. Twice a week, they would walk across town to another school to take enrichment classes.

When Chris was at school, he was quieter than he was at home. Because he was smart and liked books, kids treated him differently. He might have been picked on except for his size: by the time he reached sixth grade, the kids called him Sasquatch because, like that mythical monster (also known as Bigfoot),

The Coretta Scott King Award

Coretta Scott King spent most of her life working for civil rights, justice, equality, and peace.

Chris Curtis wasn't the only black child in the United States who wanted to read books about other kids like him. People in the Civil Rights Movement realized how important it was to have good books for kids that reflected the African-American experience.

With this in mind, the Coretta Scott King Award was established in 1970 to honor the widow of Martin Luther King, Jr. Every year, one book is chosen for the Author Award and one or more books are awarded the Honor title. The idea is to encourage writers and illustrators to create books that black children can relate to.

So far, Christopher Paul Curtis has received the Author Award twice—in 2000 for *Bud, Not Buddy*, and in 2008 for *Elijah of Buxton*. *The Watsons Go to Birmingham—1963* won the Honor title in 1996.

Some other multiple winners are Walter Dean Myers, Sharon M. Draper, Virginia Hamilton, Mildred Taylor, Angela Johnson, and Patricia C. McKissack. These are just a few of the talented African-American writers who have made sure that library shelves and bookstores now stock great books about black kids.

he had great big feet—size 13. Whenever there was a disagreement or some boys thought they'd get a little fun out of bullying him, there was only one way to work it out. "I'll see you on Friday," said Chris.

Friday was Fight Day. Every week, boys met in an out-of-the-way spot to fight. To everyone's surprise, maybe even his own, Chris was a good fighter. He lost only two fights in his life. He can remember curling up in a ball on the ground during one of those times while someone kicked him. But mostly he won.

With five lively kids in the family, there was always teasing going on. The kids tumbled and fought like a pack of puppies. When Chris was little, his sister Lindsey was twice his size and he was scared that someday she was going to kill him. He had his turn when his younger sisters and brothers came along.

Echoes

When Byron beats up Larry Dunn for stealing Kenny's gloves in The Watsons Go to Birmingham—1963, *the details are excruciatingly real, complete with sound effects and the bloodthirsty enjoyment of the crowd. Kenny, who has been a longtime victim of Larry's bullying, appreciates his brother's showmanship and sense of humor as he pounds Larry to bits. However, even though Larry is his enemy, Kenny cannot bear watching him get hurt, and he leaves.*

Echoes

A lot of the fun in The Watsons *comes from the exchanges between the kids. Byron is always making Kenny's life a misery, while Kenny does his best to keep out of his way. When asked which character is more like him, Christopher Paul Curtis answers, "Kenny, the good, sensitive, kind one," but his brothers and sisters say, "Byron, the bad one!"*

A Country in Turmoil

In 1963, racial problems exploded in the United States. That summer, Herman Curtis went to Washington, D.C., to hear Martin Luther King, Jr. give his famous "I have a dream" speech about bringing equality and justice to the world. Night after night, Chris sat with his family watching television as the violence in the South unfolded. On September 15, 1963, white racists bombed the 16th Street Baptist Church in Birmingham, Alabama, during Sunday school. Four young girls died, and others were wounded.

Chris was 10—old enough to be aware of what was going on in his country. Because of his parents' involvement in fighting prejudice, he knew about the deep divisions between black and white. The news reports of violence, riots, and the bombing of the church in Alabama all made a deep impression on Chris.

Echoes

Christopher Paul Curtis used the true story of the Alabama bombing as inspiration for his first book, The Watsons Go to Birmingham—1963. *Most of* The Watsons *is about comical, everyday events in family life, but all the paths in the story lead to the 16th Street Baptist Church. Kenny, like Chris, has to try and figure out why people hate each other so much.*

Standing Up and Speaking Out

When Chris was in middle school, his family moved to a new housing development on the edge of town. It was a big change for everyone. In a community of 190 houses, there were only three black families. School was different now. In eighth grade, only five

A Struggle for Justice

NO MORE BIRMINGHAMS

One week after the bombing of the church in Birmingham, people joined this march in Washington, D.C., to remember the four young girls who were killed.

In the 1960s, many people from both races joined together in the Civil Rights Movement to try to fix the inequalities between whites and blacks in the United States. Many of the struggles were focused on the southern states, where they battled segregation and registered African Americans to vote.

The white people who hated blacks reacted with violence. They targeted civil rights workers but they also picked random victims, trying to scare people into being quiet about injustice. Many people were beaten up; some were killed.

The Flint Public Library, where Chris began his lifelong love affair with books and libraries.

to ten percent of the kids were black, and the teachers were white. But Chris didn't have too much trouble fitting in. He was easy-going and funny, and he liked to do the unexpected. When he ran for vice-president of the student council, he spent some time thinking about how he could win. He realized that the election was all about who was popular. Musicians were popular, so he stood up and sang a song in front of the whole school. He made a big hit and he won the election.

Not everyone thought he was funny. His gym teacher didn't like him from the word *go*, and always found a way to make little comments that made Chris uncomfortable. He talked about Chris being "uppity," and referred to him and other African Americans as "you people." For the first time, Chris felt that the color of his skin made someone dislike him.

When it came time to get his marks, the gym teacher gave him the lowest mark possible for citizenship—1. Chris knew he deserved better than that. He hadn't told his parents how the teacher picked on him. Now it would all come out.

Chris knew his parents well. They weren't the type to sit back and let this kind of discrimination slide. His father went in to school with him and they both met with the gym teacher and the principal in the office. They went over the problem and then Herman gave his son the word: wait outside. Chris sat down miserably on a chair in the hall. He felt awful. He could hear his father's voice through the wall. It started out reasonable, and then gradually got louder and louder. Herman demanded answers from the gym teacher as to why he was treating his son differently from the white kids.

Finally he emerged, straightening his tie. Chris got up and they walked home together. His mark had been changed. The teacher was in trouble. Hopefully, he would think twice before he treated a black boy badly again.

Herman told Chris to come to him sooner if he was ever bullied by a teacher again. Chris agreed. But unlike the unfair mark, the effects of the episode couldn't be erased. Chris had tasted the bitterness of racial prejudice firsthand, and it stayed with him.

Echoes

The effects of racism appear in all of Curtis's books. Racial discrimination is always there, an inescapable part of his characters' lives. Elijah may be the first child born free in Buxton, but everyone around him has been touched by the horrors of slavery. The Watsons seem untouched by prejudice until their trip down south, when their parents start worrying about finding gas stations and restaurants that will serve African Americans. Later, the bombing brings the brutal reality of racism into all their lives.

The Water Fountain Spy

Chris loved reading, but just like Luther in *Bucking the Sarge*, his absolutely favorite subject at school wasn't English—it was science. However, like a lot of kids, he started losing interest in his studies when he got to high school. He got through, but he didn't shine the way he had in grade school.

Chris always liked writing stories, and he kept that up. His father got into reading books about spies, and Chris read them all too. Two of his favorite television shows were also about spies: *The Man from U.N.C.L.E.* and *Get Smart.*

Soon he started making up his own stories about spies and writing them down. There was one about a guy who worked in a bank. Everyone thought he was just a regular worker, but when no one was looking, he would turn a secret handle on the water fountain that opened a door in the wall behind it. That led to spy headquarters, and that's when the fun began.

Chris would work on these stories for a while, but then he always found they didn't work out the way he wanted them to and he put them aside. When he was 10, he told his brothers and sisters that he was going to write a novel someday, but as he grew older, this didn't seem likely.

Grown-up Life

Chris enrolled in college, but he didn't like it much. He knew if he quit he could get a job in the auto factory and make a lot of money. His mother didn't want him to leave college, but he was old enough to make his own decisions about his life.

For a while, it was great. He had his own apartment and his own car, and lots of money to spend on

When Christopher Paul Curtis finally decided to become a writer, it didn't take too long for him to realize he had made the right decision. His very first book was an instant hit.

going out and having a good time. There was only one problem: he hated the job. He was hanging 36-kilogram (80-pound) doors on cars in a hot, noisy factory he nicknamed "The Jungle." He didn't know what else to do, so he stuck to it—day after day—for 13 years.

It was very difficult for Curtis to make a change. He didn't want to give up the steady paycheck. In Canada, he met a woman named Kaysandra Sookram and he poured all his feelings for her into love letters. She thought, "Hmm, this guy sure can write!" They got married and had a little boy, Steven, and still Curtis worked in the factory.

Christopher, his daughter, Cydney, and Suki the cat.

As the years went by, Kaysandra gave him steady encouragement. She knew he could do much more than hang doors on cars. He worked out an arrangement with his partner at the factory: instead of taking turns hanging doors, they each worked steadily for 30 minutes and then had a 30-minute break while the other one hung the doors. Curtis used those breaks to write. Amid all the crashing noise, he found he was able to turn his thoughts inward and write. It made work bearable.

Writing in the Library

Curtis finally took the plunge and quit his job. The family moved to Windsor, Canada, right across the river from Detroit. They had a daughter, Cydney. He enrolled in some university courses, including creative writing classes. He won a couple of writing contests and then, with Kaysandra's enthusiastic support, he took a year off to write a book. Every morning, he went to the children's section in the Windsor Public Library and wrote. The library made him feel peaceful and happy, just like on those Saturdays long ago in Flint.

His son, Steven, now a teenager, helped him by typing out his work at night and telling him what was working and what wasn't.

At the end of the year, Curtis entered his manuscript in a publisher's contest. He didn't win, but the publisher liked his book so much they decided to publish it anyway. *The Watsons Go to Birmingham—1963* was an instant hit, winning two very big awards: the Coretta Scott King Honor Award and the Newbery Honor Book.

With this funny, engaging tale of a family from Flint who drive down to Birmingham during the racially troubled 1960s, Curtis proved he could write. The family was a lot like his own. Kenny, the hero, was 10, the same age Curtis was the year of the bombing in Birmingham. However, even though *The Watsons* was successful, Curtis still had to work at odd jobs for a while to make a living.

But not for long. *Bud, Not Buddy* was an even bigger hit. *Bud* won the Newbery Medal AND the Coretta Scott King Author Award, and Curtis was established as a full-time, very successful children's author.

Christopher Paul Curtis continues to write books in which he uses his sense of mischief and fun to create irresistible characters

To create this kind of magic, a writer needs a very special kind of imagination.

Curtis says *Elijah of Buxton* was his favorite book to write because the character and the story came to him right away, ready to go.

and laugh-out-loud situations. But underneath the humor and the adventure, he addresses the core issues about what it has meant to be black in America over the last 200 years.

These days, Curtis has moved to the local university library to do his writing. But he still likes to go back to his old spot in the children's section at the Windsor Public Library to write a few pages, just for old times' sake. And when he's nearly finished, he makes a pilgrimage across the U.S.–Canada border to Detroit and drives for an hour back to his hometown, and the Flint Public Library on Kearsley Street. He finds a quiet desk in the children's section, where he can see the big trees out the window, and puts the final touches on the manuscript. "I guess I'm a little superstitious," he says. "But that's where it all began."

BOOKS

Christopher Paul Curtis has written three books for kids aged 9 to 12.

The Watsons Go to Birmingham—1963
Bud, Not Buddy
Elijah of Buxton

The following book is for older readers, 12 and up.

Bucking the Sarge

These two are picture books for younger readers.

Mr. Chickee's Messy Mission
Mr. Chickee's Funny Money

Judy Levin has written a very detailed biography, titled *Christopher Paul Curtis*, which includes an interview with the author by some fourth-grade students.

Selected Bibliography

Lucy Maud Montgomery

Gammel, Irene. *Looking for Anne: How Lucy Maud Montgomery Dreamed Up a Literary Classic.* Key Porter. Toronto, 2008.

Montgomery, L. M. *The Alpine Path: The Story of My Career.* Fitzhenry and Whiteside. Toronto, 1917.

Montgomery, L. M. *The Selected Journals of L. M. Montgomery. Volume I: 1889–1910.* Edited by Mary Rubio and Elizabeth Waterston. Oxford University Press. Toronto, 1985.

Rubio, Mary, and Elizabeth Waterston. *Writing a Life: L. M. Montgomery.* ECW Press. Toronto, 1995.

C. S. Lewis

Gopnik, Adam. "Prisoner of Narnia: How C. S. Lewis Escaped." *The New Yorker,* November 21, 2005.

Green, Roger Lancelyn, and Walter Hooper. *C. S. Lewis: A Biography.* HarperCollins Publishers. London, 1974.

Lewis, C. S. *The Collected Letters of C. S. Lewis. Volume I: Family Letters 1905–1931.* Edited by Walter Hooper. HarperCollins. New York, 2004.

Lewis, C. S. *Surprised by Joy: The Shape of My Early Life.* Geoffrey Bles. London, 1955.

Sayer, George. *Jack: C. S. Lewis and His Times.* Harper and Row. San Francisco, 1988.

E. B. White

Elledge, Scott. *E. B. White: A Biography.* W.W. Norton. New York, 1984.

White, E. B. *The Letters of E. B. White.* Collected and edited by Dorothy Lobrano Guth. Harper & Row. New York, 1976.

Madeleine L'Engle

Chase, Carole F. *Suncatcher: A Study of Madeleine L'Engle and Her Writing.* Second Edition. Innisfree Press. Philadelphia, 1998.

Hettinga, Donald. *Presenting Madeleine L'Engle.* Twayne Publishers. New York, 1993.

L'Engle, Madeleine. *A Circle of Quiet.* Farrar, Straus and Giroux. New York, 1972.

Zarin, Cynthia. "The Storyteller." *The New Yorker.* April 12, 2004.

Philip Pullman

Moreton, Cole. "His Dark Materials." *The Independent.* May 25, 2008.

Parkin, Lance, and Mark Jones. *Dark Matters.* Virgin Books. London, 2005.

Pullman, Philip. Official website: http://www.philip-pullman.com.

Rabinovitch, Dina. "His Bright Materials." *The Guardian.* December 10, 2003.

Tucker, Nicholas. *Darkness Visible: Inside the World of Philip Pullman.* Wizard Books. Cambridge, 2003.

Christopher Paul Curtis

Bailey, Laura. "The Bard of Flint." *Michigan Today.* Fall 2006.

Levin, Judy. *Christopher Paul Curtis.* Rosen Publishing Group. New York, 2006.

Notes

Page 24   *"... amid all the commonplaces of life ..."* L. M. Montgomery, *The Alpine Path: The Story of My Career* (Toronto: Fitzhenry and Whiteside, 1917), 48.

Page 28   *"I cannot remember the time ..."* L. M. Montgomery, *The Alpine Path: The Story of My Career* (Toronto: Fitzhenry and Whiteside, 1917), 52.

Page 43   *"There were books in the study ..."* C. S. Lewis, *Surprised by Joy: The Shape of My Early Life* (London: Geoffrey Bles, 1955), 17.

Page 50   *"With my mother's death all settled happiness ..."* C. S. Lewis, *Surprised by Joy: The Shape of My Early Life* (London: Geoffrey Bles, 1955), 27.

Page 72   *"The barn was very large ..."* E. B. White, *Charlotte's Web* (New York: HarperCollins, 1952), 13.

Page 85   *"Life in the barn was very good ..."* E. B. White, *Charlotte's Web* (New York: HarperCollins, 1952), 183.

Page 92   *"My real life was not in school ..."* Madeleine L'Engle as quoted by Doreen Gonzales in *Madeleine L'Engle: Author of A Wrinkle in Time* (New York: Macmillan, 1991), 24.

Page 127   *"When I first became aware that ..."* Philip Pullman, official website: http://www.philip-pullman.com.

Index

Note: Book titles starting with "A" and "The" are listed under the next word. For example, *The Golden Compass* is under "G."

We acknowledge the support of the Canada Council for the Arts, the Government of
Canada through the Book Publishing Industry Development Program (BPIDP) for our
publishing activities, and the Ontario Arts Council.

ONTARIO ARTS COUNCIL
CONSEIL DES ARTS DE L'ONTARIO

Cataloging in Publication
Cotter, Charis
        Born to write : the remarkable lives of six famous authors / by Charis Cotter.

Includes bibliographical references and index.
ISBN 978-1-55451-192-1 (bound).—ISBN 978-1-55451-191-4 (pbk.)

        1. Authors—Biography—Juvenile literature. I. Title.

PN452.C68 2009   j809   C2009-902865-4

Distributed in Canada by: Published in the U.S.A. by:

Firefly Books Ltd.   Annick Press (U.S.) Ltd.
66 Leek Crescent   Distributed in the U.S.A. by:
Richmond Hill, ON   Firefly Books (U.S.) Inc.
L4B 1H1   P.O. Box 1338
                                   Ellicott Station
                                   Buffalo, NY 14205

Printed in China.

Visit us at: www.annickpress.com
Visit Charis Cotter at: www.chariscotter.com